Defensive Plays

D & B Publishing

New and forthcoming books.

D & B Poker

1-904468-06-3	*Poker on the Internet*	Andrew Kinsman
1-904468-08-X	*How Good is your Pot-Limit Hold'em?*	Stewart Reuben
1-904468-07-1	*How Good is your Pot-Limit Omaha?*	Stewart Reuben

D & B Bridge

1-904468-01-2	*Suit Contracts*	Brian Senior
1-904468-00-4	*No-trump Contracts*	David Bird

D & B Puzzles

1-904468-03-9	*200 Word Puzzles*	Carter and Russell
1-904468-02-0	*400 IQ Puzzles*	Carter and Russell
1-904468-10-1	*Solving IQ Puzzles*	Carter and Russell
1-904468-11-X	*Solving Word Puzzles*	Carter and Russell
1-904468-05-5	The Times *Two Brains*	Keene and Jacobs

D & B General

1-904468-13-6	*Online Gambling*	Angus Dunnington

D & B Publishing, PO Box 18, Hassocks, West Sussex BN6 9WR, UK
Tel: 01273 834680, Fax: 01273 831629, e-mail: info@dandbpublishing.com.
Website: www.dandbpublishing.com

defensive plays

Sally Brock

D&B PUBLISHING
www.dandbpublishing.com

First published in 2003 by D & B Publishing, PO Box 18, Hassocks, West
Sussex BN6 9WR

British Library Cataloguing-in-Publication Data
A catalogue record for this book is available from the British Library.

ISBN 1-904468-09-8

All sales enquiries should be directed to:
D & B Publishing, PO Box 18, Hassocks, West Sussex BN6 9WR, UK
Tel: 01273 834680, Fax: 01273 831629, e-mail: info@dandbpublishing.com,
Website: www.dandbpublishing.com

Cover design by Horatio Monteverde.
Production by Wakewing Ltd, High Wycombe.
Printed and bound in Great Britain by Biddles Ltd.

Contents

Introduction

Defence is generally considered to be the hardest, yet ultimately the most rewarding, aspect of bridge. This is because, in addition to all the other difficulties, the two players who are supposed to be working together cannot see each other's cards. And, of course, it is particularly important to become a good defender because you defend twice as often as you play the hand. Bearing this in mind, it is extraordinary how many beginners' books have many more chapters on declarer play than on defence.

There are two main elements to defence: first, try to build up a picture of the unseen hands; and second, form a plan to defeat the contract based on that picture.

You can use several tools to help you build your picture: the bidding, partner's opening lead, partner's signal on your opening lead, declarer's early play, etc. The longer you can postpone the key play, the more information you will have received. Sometimes you can build only a partial picture and will have to guess the rest, but that should be an informed guess.

The opening lead style assumed in these pages is fourth highest from honours, second highest from three or more small cards (see page 42 for what to play on the second round) and top of a doubleton; we lead the top of touching honours.

The aim of this book is to show you some of the tools that are available to the defenders, and then to give you plenty of opportunities – via a total of 100 defensive problems – to practise them for yourself. One thing is for sure: when you have finished this book you will be a better defender than when you started.

Sally Brock

June 2003

To Raymond
Without whose love and hard work
nothing would be possible

Chapter One

Basic Signalling

- **Attitude**
- **Count**
- **Another Convention in Defensive Play**
- **Suit Preference**
- **What Card to Return**

You have no chance of working out how to defend accurately unless you can build up a picture of the two hidden hands. The bidding and the sight of dummy will help you do this to some extent, but further vital information can be exchanged by *signalling*.

Signalling means playing cards in a particular way in order to impart specific information. As well as being an important aspect of defence in the real world, the method of signalling I am going to describe here will help you to get value from this book.

There are countless varieties of signalling in the tournament world, but what I intend to explain here is the most common form in the UK. It is what I call 'normal' and is what you would expect if playing with a stranger without discussion. Of course, regular partnerships often introduce refinements or do something different altogether.

Attitude

Attitude signals are generally played on partner's lead.

An *attitude* signal is one that attempts to tell partner if you would like him to continue the suit he has led or if you would prefer he try something else. **Attitude signals are generally played on partner's lead.** The 'normal' style is to play a high card to encourage and a low card to discourage. (If you play in tournaments you may come across some pairs playing 'reverse', where the opposite is true.)

Suppose partner leads an ace. Dummy has three small cards and you hold 9-6-2. You play your lowest card, showing no interest in the suit. On the other hand, if you hold Q-6-2 you play the six, encouraging partner to continue.

Against a suit contract a high card can also indicate a desire to ruff. So suppose partner leads the ace of a side-suit; dummy has, say, J-7-3 and you hold 8-4: against no-trumps you would play the four to discourage, but against a suit contract you would play the eight, hoping partner would continue the suit and give you a ruff.

It is important to signal encouragement with the highest card you can afford. Remember that partner will usually not have perfect knowledge about your spot cards. If you play an in-between card because you are not quite sure whether or not you want partner to continue the suit, all you are likely to convey is uncertainty about your original holding.

Count

Count signals are generally played on declarer's lead.

A *count* signal is one that attempts to show partner how many cards you hold in the suit. **Count signals are generally played on declarer's lead**, or on partner's lead when attitude is already known (say partner leads the ace and Q-J-x appears in the dummy). A high card followed by a lower one denotes an even number; when cards are played upwards an odd number is suggested. If declarer plays the king from his hand and there is Q-J-10-6 in the dummy, you play the eight from 9-8-5-4 but the four from 9-5-4 (again, some tournament players do the reverse).

In a count situation the recommended procedure is to peter (i.e. play high-low) by playing your second highest card first (or top of a doubleton) – sometimes partner will be able to tell from the spot cards he can see that you cannot have four. In the example given above, if you played the five under declarer's king, partner would not know whether you started with 9-8-5-4 or 9-8-5 with declarer holding the four.

Another Convention in Defensive Play

Play the lowest of touching honours to force out declarer's high cards.

Suppose partner leads the two of hearts. Dummy holds 9-7-3 and you hold Q-J-4. Which card do you play at trick one? The answer is that you should play the jack, the lower of touching honours, whether you are defending no-trumps or a suit contract. There is a very good reason for this. Suppose partner has led from K-8-6-2. If you play the jack and declarer wins the ace, partner *knows* that you hold the queen, for if declarer held it he would surely win with it. However, if you played the queen and declarer won the ace, then partner would not know who held the jack.

Suit-preference Signals

A suit-preference signal is one that asks partner to play a particular suit.

A suit-preference signal is one that asks partner to play a particular suit. These are used only in a few specific situations. The most common use of suit-preference signals is when you know that partner is going to ruff the card that you play. In these circumstances if you play a high card you are asking him to play next the higher-ranking of the remaining two suits (not trumps) and if you play a low card you are asking him to return the lower-ranking suit. A middle card shows no preference between the remaining two suits.

As we will see later, this concept can be extended to cover other situations where count and attitude are already known, or else deemed to be relatively unimportant.

Which Card to Return

We all know that we should lead fourth highest from long suits, but if partner wins the trick and returns the suit, which card should he play? Consider this situation:

When returning partner's suit, lead your top card from an original three-card holding, or your original fourth highest from a longer suit.

87

K 10 6 5 2   ☐☐☐☐☐☐☐

You lead the five against a no-trump contract. Partner wins the ace as declarer plays the four. Partner now continues with the three and declarer plays the queen. Suppose you have no outside entry; should you play the king, hoping that partner started out with A-J-9-3, or should you duck, expecting partner to have begun with A-9-3?

The answer here is that you should win and continue the suit to partner's jack. The reason is that partner should return his original fourth highest from a long suit, but his highest remaining card from an original three-card holding. So when he plays the three, you know that he started with either a doubleton or a four-card suit and you have to hope it was the latter.

Of course, had he returned the nine, you would have known that he could not have a four-card suit, so unless you had a sure entry you would have ducked declarer's queen, hoping that partner would get in later and continue the suit.

Try it Yourself

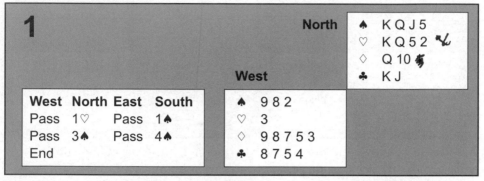

1

			North	♠ K Q J 5
				♡ K Q 5 2
				◊ Q 10
			West	♣ K J

West	North	East	South	♠ 9 8 2
Pass	1♡	Pass	1♠	♡ 3
Pass	3♠	Pass	4♠	◊ 9 8 7 5 3
End				♣ 8 7 5 4

You, West, lead your singleton heart against South's 4♠. Your partner wins the ace, declarer playing the ♡4, and returns the ♡6, declarer playing the ♡10. You ruff, but what do you play next?

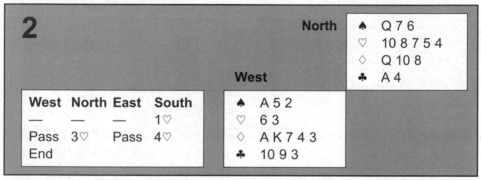

2

			North	♠ Q 7 6
				♡ 10 8 7 5 4
				◊ Q 10 8
			West	♣ A 4

West	North	East	South	♠ A 5 2
—	—	—	1♡	♡ 6 3
Pass	3♡	Pass	4♡	◊ A K 7 4 3
End				♣ 10 9 3

You, West, lead the ◊A and partner plays the ◊9 as declarer plays the ◊J. How do you defend?

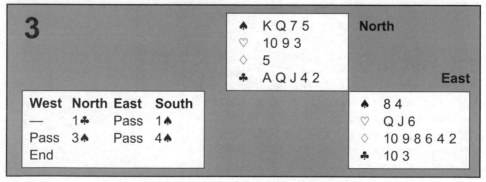

3

♠ K Q 7 5	North	
♡ 10 9 3		
◊ 5		
♣ A Q J 4 2		**East**

West	North	East	South	♠ 8 4
—	1♣	Pass	1♠	♡ Q J 6
Pass	3♠	Pass	4♠	◊ 10 9 8 6 4 2
End				♣ 10 3

You partner leads the ♡4 against South's 4♠. Declarer plays the ♡10 from dummy. What do you play?

4

	♠ 10 5 3	North
	♡ Q 6	
	◇ J 10 9 7 6 5	
	♣ 6 4	East

West	North	East	South
—	—	Pass	2♣
Pass	2◇	Pass	2NT
Pass	3NT	End	

East hand:
♠ J 9
♡ J 10 9 4 3
◇ A K 2
♣ J 8 7

West leads the ♠6. You play the ♠9, which holds the trick. You continue with the ♠J, won by declarer's ace, partner playing the ♠2. Declarer now plays the ◇Q, your partner contributing the ◇8. Plan the defence.

5

	♠ Q J 9 8 5	North
	♡ Q	
	◇ A K J	
	♣ A Q 8 2	East

West	North	East	South
—	1♠	Pass	4♡
End			

East hand:
♠ A 6 3
♡ A 7 6
◇ Q 7
♣ K J 10 7 6

Partner leads the ♣4, which is won by dummy's ace, declarer playing the ♣5. He then cashes the ◇A-K, discarding a club, and then plays the ◇J, ruffed by you and overruffed. A heart to dummy's queen and you are in. Plan the defence.

6

	North	♠ J 6
		♡ K 9
		◇ A K Q J 9 4 2
	West	♣ A 7

West	North	East	South
—	2◇*	Pass	2NT**
Pass	3NT	End	
*strong	**negative		

West hand:
♠ K 9 7 4 2
♡ J 7 3
◇ 8 3
♣ K Q 5

You lead the ♠4, won by partner with the ♠A. Partner returns the ♠8, ♠Q from declarer. How do you defend?

Solutions

1 Partner's ♡6 is his lowest heart, so he is asking you to switch to a club. If you do so, he will win his ace and give you a second heart ruff to beat declarer's game.

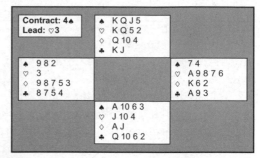

2 Don't let declarer fool you. If his ◊J is a true card, partner's diamond holding would be 9-6-5-2 and he would have not have encouraged. No, partner must have a doubleton diamond and you can give him a ruff to beat 4♡. Continue with the ◊K and ◊7, asking him to play a spade after he has made his ruff.

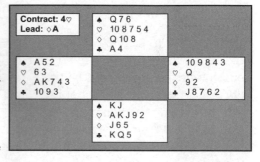

3 This hand demonstrates the importance of playing the lower of two touching honours in this position. If you play your ♡Q on this trick, when partner gets in with the ◊A he will not know that you have the jack (in fact, he will think that you have denied it). He may cash the ♡K, but will then

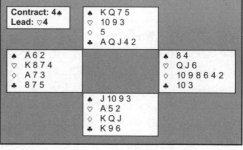

probably switch to a club, hoping to find you with the ♣K. However, if you play the ♡J at trick one, partner will *know* that you have the ♡Q too, because declarer would hardly win with the ♡A when he also had the ♡Q.

4 If you win this diamond trick and switch to a club as partner has suggested, declarer will win and play a second diamond. Whether you win or duck, he can later cross to dummy with the ♡Q to cash the established diamonds. What you must do is duck the *first* diamond,

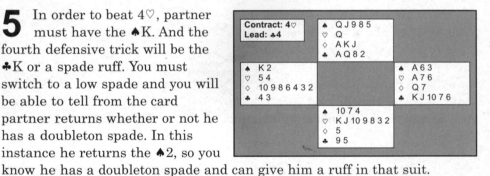

Contract: 3NT	♠ 10 5 3
Lead: ♠6	♡ Q 6
	◇ J 10 9 7 6 5
	♣ 6 4

♠ Q 8 7 6 2
♡ 8 5
◇ 8 4
♣ Q 9 5 2

♠ J 9
♡ J 10 9 4 3
◇ A K 2
♣ J 8 7

♠ A K 4
♡ A K 7 2
◇ Q 3
♣ A K 10 3

hoping that declarer has only a doubleton (and that partner's eight is the start of a peter rather than a singleton). Win the diamond continuation and play a club. Now declarer can cross to dummy with the ♡Q, but the diamonds are not established and he must go one down.

5 In order to beat 4♡, partner must have the ♠K. And the fourth defensive trick will be the ♣K or a spade ruff. You must switch to a low spade and you will be able to tell from the card partner returns whether or not he has a doubleton spade. In this instance he returns the ♠2, so you

Contract: 4♡	♠ Q J 9 8 5
Lead: ♣4	♡ Q
	◇ A K J
	♣ A Q 8 2

♠ K 2
♡ 5 4
◇ 10 9 8 6 4 3 2
♣ 4 3

♠ A 6 3
♡ A 7 6
◇ Q 7
♣ K J 10 7 6

♠ 10 7 4
♡ K J 10 9 8 3 2
◇ 5
♣ 9 5

know he has a doubleton spade and can give him a ruff in that suit.

6 Partner would not have returned the ♠8 from an original holding of A-10-8-3, so declarer's queen must be a false card. You know you cannot cash the spade suit and you know declarer has at least nine tricks if you let him in. Your only chance is in hearts. Switch to the ♡3 and hope that partner has the ace and queen.

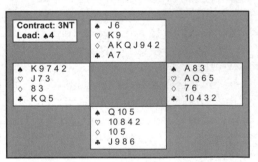

Contract: 3NT	♠ J 6
Lead: ♠4	♡ K 9
	◇ A K Q J 9 4 2
	♣ A 7

♠ K 9 7 4 2
♡ J 7 3
◇ 8 3
♣ K Q 5

♠ A 8 3
♡ A Q 6 5
◇ 7 6
♣ 10 4 3 2

♠ Q 10 5
♡ 10 8 4 2
◇ 10 5
♣ J 9 8 6

Chapter Two

Basic Plays

- **Second Hand Low**
- **Third Hand High**
- **The Rule of Eleven**

There are several basic guidelines to defensive play that offer good advice most of the time. Although there are plenty of exceptions which we will deal with later on (see *Chapter Six*), when you are starting out the following advice should help.

Second Hand Low

This means that when you are the second hand to play, i.e. in the standard diagram:

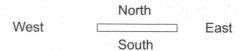

you are East and declarer plays from dummy (North), or you are West and declarer plays from his hand (South), you should generally play low. This is because your partner is still there to beat the card played by third hand. Suppose this is the layout:

```
                    7 6 2
    A 10 4        [=========]        K 9 3
                    Q J 8 5
```

> **Use your honours to capture other honours**

When declarer plays the two from the dummy, if you play your king it will hold the trick. Now declarer can make two tricks in this suit without having to cross to dummy again. On the other hand, if you play low, declarer plays the jack and partner wins the ace. Now, in order to avoid losing three tricks in the suit, declarer must cross to dummy to lead the suit again. He will need to use up an entry to do this, an entry that he could perhaps have put to another use.

Here is another example:

```
                    7 6 2
    J 10 4        [=========]        A 9 3
                    K Q 8 5
```

If you go in with the ace when declarer plays low from the dummy, he does not need to go to dummy again in order to establish tricks in this suit, so he can use his entries for something else. If you play low, he must cross to dummy again if he is to enjoy this suit.

Let us change the layout slightly:

```
                    7 6 2
    J 8 4         [=========]        A 9 3
                    K Q 10 5
```

Now when declarer plays low from dummy, you play low and declarer plays the king while you notice your partner's four, showing an odd number. Declarer crosses to dummy again and plays another low card. It can do you no harm to play low again and if you do this smoothly declarer may well play the ten, hoping you have the jack.

Third Hand High

> If your honours cannot win tricks, they may promote tricks for partner.

This means that when you are third to play, i.e. when your partner has led to the trick, you should generally play high. Suppose this is the layout:

$$7\,6\,2$$
$$K\,10\,8\,4 \qquad \boxed{} \qquad Q\,9\,3$$
$$A\,J\,5$$

If partner leads the four of this suit you should play the queen. This will force declarer's ace and now partner's king-ten is poised to take two tricks over declarer's jack. If you were to play the nine at trick one, then declarer would make a cheap trick with his jack.

It is just as important to play a high card when there is an honour in dummy. Maybe this is the layout:

$$A\,6\,2$$
$$K\,10\,8\,4 \qquad \boxed{} \qquad Q\,9\,3$$
$$J\,7\,5$$

Again, if you, third hand, play low declarer will make a trick with his jack (or seven). If you play the queen it will hold the trick and now you return the nine (the higher of two remaining cards). Whatever declarer does he can make only one trick in the suit.

The Rule of Eleven

The Rule of Eleven is a mathematical consequence of playing fourth highest leads. It helps both the defender not on opening lead and declarer to know what card they should play at trick one.

To quote the *Official Encyclopedia of Bridge*: **Subtract the pips on the card led from 11; the result gives the number of higher cards than the one led in the other three hands.**

I should stress that it only works when the lead has been fourth highest. If your opponents are playing third and fifth highest, then you need to apply the Rule of Twelve or Ten respectively.

Here is an example of the Rule of Eleven:

```
                        10 6 5
      Q 8 7 4 2   [            ]      K 3
                        A J 9
```

When West leads the four, both East and South can work out that there are seven (11 − 4) cards higher than the four in the other three hands. There are three in the dummy. So East knows that South has three cards higher than the four, and South knows that East has one card higher than the four.

'So what?' do I hear you say? Well, there are some situations where the Rule of Eleven can be invaluable.

```
                        J 5 4
      K 10 8 6 2   [            ]      Q 9 7
                        A 3
```

| Remember to check the Rule of Eleven. |

When West leads the six and declarer plays low from dummy, East can work out that declarer has only one card higher than the six. While it is possible that West started with A-K-8-6-2 and five tricks can be cashed immediately, the above layout is more likely and to play the queen would set up dummy's jack as a second stopper in the suit.

The Rule of Eleven can also help both sides realise that the lead has been second highest from a poor suit rather than fourth highest at all.

```
                        A Q 9
      8 6 4 2     [            ]      K 10
                        J 7 5 3
```

West leads the six against a no-trump contract. Declarer can see five cards higher in his two combined hands, so plays the nine from the dummy. East, hoping that partner has led from J-8-7-6(-x), plays the ten. Now declarer knows that West has not led from K-10-8-6(-x), so he may well have led from 8-6-x-x, in which case East's king will drop on the next round.

Try it Yourself

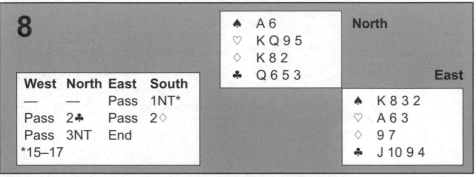

7

West	North	East	South
—	—	—	1NT*
Pass	2♣	Pass	2♡
Pass	3♡	Pass	4♡
End			
*15–17			

North
- ♠ 6 5
- ♡ K Q 10 4
- ♢ Q J 5
- ♣ J 7 6 2

East
- ♠ K 10 4
- ♡ 9 8 7
- ♢ A 6 4
- ♣ 10 5 4 3

West leads the ♠3. Declarer plays low from dummy. What do you play?

8

West	North	East	South
—	—	Pass	1NT*
Pass	2♣	Pass	2♢
Pass	3NT	End	
*15–17			

North
- ♠ A 6
- ♡ K Q 9 5
- ♢ K 8 2
- ♣ Q 6 5 3

East
- ♠ K 8 3 2
- ♡ A 6 3
- ♢ 9 7
- ♣ J 10 9 4

West leads the ♠J and declarer plays the six from dummy. What do you play?

9

North
- ♠ Q 8 2
- ♡ J 9 7 3
- ♢ Q J 10
- ♣ J 10 2

West
- ♠ K 9 4
- ♡ A 8
- ♢ A 6 5 4 2
- ♣ 8 6 3

West	North	East	South
—	Pass	Pass	1♡
Pass	2♡	3♣	Pass
Pass	3♡	End	

You, West, lead the ♣6. Dummy plays low and partner's ♣9 forces declarer's ace. Declarer plays the ♡K which you win, and you play the ♣8 to partner's queen and declarer ruffs. He now draws one more round of trumps and plays a diamond to dummy's queen and another diamond which you win with the ace. He ruffs your club continuation and plays a low spade. Over to you.

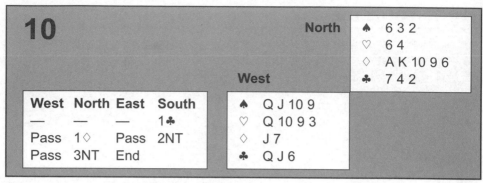

10

North

♠ 6 3 2
♡ 6 4
◇ A K 10 9 6
♣ 7 4 2

West

West	North	East	South
—	—	—	1♣
Pass	1◇	Pass	2NT
Pass	3NT	End	

♠ Q J 10 9
♡ Q 10 9 3
◇ J 7
♣ Q J 6

At trick one you lead the ♠Q, which holds, partner playing the ♠7. You continue with the ♠9 to partner's king and he plays a third spade won by declarer's ♠A. Declarer now plays the ◇4. Plan the defence.

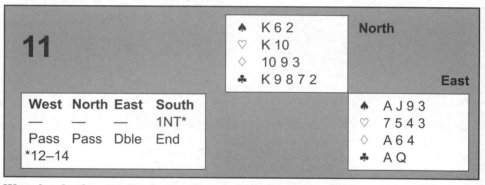

11

♠ K 6 2
♡ K 10
◇ 10 9 3
♣ K 9 8 7 2

North

West	North	East	South
—	—	—	1NT*
Pass	Pass	Dble	End
*12–14			

East

♠ A J 9 3
♡ 7 5 4 3
◇ A 6 4
♣ A Q

West leads the ♠7. Declarer plays low from dummy. What do you play?

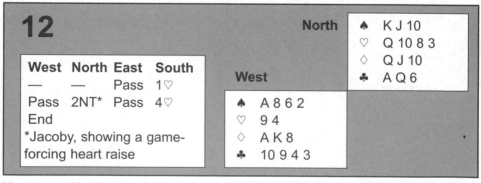

12

North

♠ K J 10
♡ Q 10 8 3
◇ Q J 10
♣ A Q 6

West	North	East	South
—	—	Pass	1♡
Pass	2NT*	Pass	4♡
End			
*Jacoby, showing a game-forcing heart raise			

West

♠ A 8 6 2
♡ 9 4
◇ A K 8
♣ 10 9 4 3

You start off with ◇A-K-8, partner playing the ◇7, ◇2 and ◇5. Declarer wins the third round in dummy, plays a heart to his ace and the ♠4. What do you do?

Solutions

7 Against a suit contract your partner should very rarely underleada an ace, so if you play your ♠K it will be headed by declarer's ace. This knowledge makes some inexperienced players withhold their king in this type of position. But this deal shows what a mistake that would be. As long as

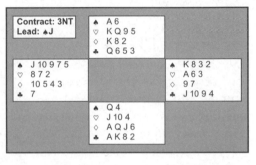

Contract: 4♡	♠ 6 5
Lead: ♠3	♡ K Q 10 4
	◇ Q J 5
	♣ J 7 6 2

♠ Q 9 8 3		♠ K 10 4
♡ 3 2		♡ 9 8 7
◇ K 9 7 2		◇ A 6 4
♣ K 9 8		♣ 10 5 4 3

	♠ A J 7 2
	♡ A J 6 5
	◇ 10 8 3
	♣ A Q

you play your king of spades, the defence must come to one spade, two diamonds and a club, while if you let declarer win trick one cheaply with the jack, you will have reduced the number of defensive winners to three.

8 You should play your ♠K. You do not know whether partner has four or five spades (he can't have only three for you know declarer does not have a four-card major). If he has four it does not matter much, but if he has five it is vital that you take your king now; then declarer's ace and queen will fall on the same trick.

Contract: 3NT	♠ A 6
Lead: ♠J	♡ K Q 9 5
	◇ K 8 2
	♣ Q 6 5 3

♠ J 10 9 7 5		♠ K 8 3 2
♡ 8 7 2		♡ A 6 3
◇ 10 5 4 3		◇ 9 7
♣ 7		♣ J 10 9 4

	♠ Q 4
	♡ J 10 4
	◇ A Q J 6
	♣ A K 8 2

9 It is important that you play a low spade on this trick. If declarer has the ♠A he is cold for ten tricks and the opponents have missed a game, so you must play your partner for that card. If you go in with the ♠K – which is a very common error – declarer will lose only two tricks when he has the unsupported jack in hand. However, if you play low he will play dummy's

Contract: 3♡	♠ Q 8 2
Lead: ♣6	♡ J 9 7 3
	◇ Q J 10
	♣ J 10 2

♠ K 9 4		♠ A 10 6
♡ A 8		♡ 5 4
◇ A 6 5 4 2		◇ 8 7
♣ 8 6 3		♣ K Q 9 7 5 4

	♠ J 7 5 3
	♡ K Q 10 6 2
	◇ K 9 3
	♣ A

queen, which your partner will win with the ace. Partner can now return the ♠10, which declarer will cover with the jack, and your king and nine will both score.

10 If you play a low diamond and declarer plays the ◇10, partner is in a difficult position. If he wins his ◇Q, declarer will make nine tricks – one spade, two hearts, four diamonds and two clubs. On the other hand, if partner ducks dummy's ◇10 then declarer should

Contract: 3NT Lead: ♠Q	♠ 6 3 2 ♡ 6 4 ◇ A K 10 9 6 ♣ 7 4 2	
♠ Q J 10 9 ♡ Q 10 9 3 ◇ J 7 ♣ Q J 6		♠ K 7 4 ♡ J 7 2 ◇ Q 8 3 2 ♣ 10 8 3
	♠ A 8 5 ♡ A K 8 5 ◇ 5 4 ♣ A K 9 5	

proceed by ducking a club, which will also result in nine tricks: one spade, two hearts, three diamonds and three clubs. Best defence is to put in the ◇J on the first round of the suit, holding declarer to only two diamond tricks. Now if declarer ducks, you cash your long spade and exit with a diamond, cutting the communications between dummy and declarer's hand.

11 Use your Rule of Eleven. If you subtract seven from eleven you get four, and you can see four cards higher than the seven in dummy and your own hand. If partner has led fourth highest, the seven will hold (and if not it does not matter much which card you play). Partner can now lead a

Contract: 1NT doubled Lead: ♠7	♠ K 6 2 ♡ K 10 ◇ 10 9 3 ♣ K 9 8 7 2	
♠ Q 10 8 7 ♡ 9 8 2 ◇ 8 7 5 ♣ 6 5 3		♠ A J 9 3 ♡ 7 5 4 3 ◇ A 6 4 ♣ A Q
	♠ 5 4 ♡ A Q J 6 ◇ K Q J 2 ♣ J 10 4	

second spade through dummy's king. A word of warning, though. It is important that partner plays a club when he gets in with the fourth round of spades and he might not realise the importance of doing this. When you win a spade, switch to the ♡7, so partner realises that you have nothing in that suit. Then, when you get in with the ◇A, you can cash any remaining spade tricks, leaving partner on lead, and he will know to play a club.

12 Declarer is trying to panic you into going in with the ♠A and stop him needing a guess. You should be suspicious of his play. His failure to take a heart finesse suggests that he has the ace-king in the suit, and he needs the ♣K to make up his opening bid. The only card your partner can have that is

Contract: 4♡ Lead: ◇A	♠ K J 10 ♡ Q 10 8 3 ◇ Q J 10 ♣ A Q 6	
♠ A 8 6 2 ♡ 9 4 ◇ A K 8 ♣ 10 9 4 3		♠ Q 9 7 5 ♡ 7 5 ◇ 9 7 5 2 ♣ 8 7 2
	♠ 4 3 ♡ A K J 6 2 ◇ 6 4 3 ♣ K J 5	

of any use is the ♠Q, so play low smoothly and hope declarer guesses wrong.

Chapter Three

Active or Passive?

An active defence is one where you lead from honours, hoping to promote your side's defensive tricks before declarer has established sufficient tricks of his own. The problem is that sometimes such an attack can set up winners for declarer that he would otherwise have been unable to make.

A passive defence simply tries not to give declarer any tricks that were not his by right. The problem is that sometimes this allows declarer to set up his own tricks before the defence's tricks are established.

The first time you should ask yourself the 'Active or Passive?' question is when you are selecting your opening lead. Simply put, the more confident the opponents' auction and the better placed you think the defensive cards are for them, the more attacking should be your lead.

Let's give a couple of examples. Suppose the bidding goes
1♡ − 1♠ − 1NT − 3NT, and you hold:

♠ K J 4
♡ 8 7 6
◇ K J 4 3
♣ J 10 4

Lead a diamond. Your spades look well placed for declarer,
partner's hearts look well placed for declarer, and your
opponents seem to have plenty of high-card points. Maybe
this is the full deal:

Attack if the opponents sound confident or if the cards sit badly for you.	

If you don't cash your diamond suit declarer might make as
many as thirteen tricks. Of course, they could have made Four
Spades, but that is no reason to let them make Three No-
trumps.

Play safe if the opponents crawl into their contract and the cards lie badly for declarer.	Now consider the opposite position. This time the bidding goes 1♡ − 1♠ − 1NT − 2NT − 3NT and you hold: ♠ 5 4 ♡ K J 10 4 ◇ A J 4 3 ♣ J 10 4 Here your hearts lie badly for declarer and hopefully partner's spades lie over dummy's strength. In addition, the opponents have told you that they do not have a lot of points to spare. The last thing you want to do is give them anything

to which they are not entitled. Here I would recommend leading the jack of clubs. Perhaps the full deal is:

	North	
♠ A J 9 7 3		
♡ 8 2		
◇ Q 10 7		
♣ Q 7 6		

West

♠ 5 4	♠ K Q 8 2
♡ K J 10 4	♡ 7 6 5
◇ A J 4 3	◇ 6 5
♣ J 10 4	♣ 9 8 3 2

East

	South
♠ 10 6	
♡ A Q 9 3	
◇ K 9 8 2	
♣ A K 5	

In the middle of the hand lead low from an honour and high from small cards.

On a club lead declarer will surely win in hand and run the ten of spades. Best defence now is a high heart switch from East, probably ducked to West, who will continue with another club. Declarer's natural line is to win and take a second spade finesse, and East will play another heart through. There is no way for declarer to make his contract.

Now consider the play on a more active diamond lead. Declarer does best to win in hand and return a diamond to dummy's ten, followed by the queen of diamonds. Suppose you win the ace and switch to a club. Declarer wins the ace, cashes the king of diamonds and runs the ten of spades. This is the position:

Unless you have a positive plan, avoid switching to new suits – it is said to cost half a trick a time!

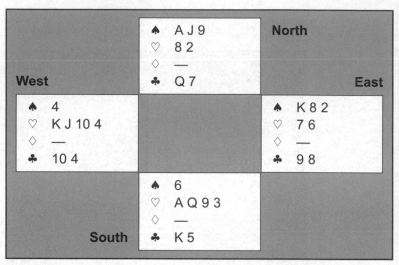

Suppose East returns the seven of hearts to the three and West's ten. Whatever West returns, declarer can safely lose another spade to East, setting up the jack for his ninth trick.

The above examples are concerned with the opening lead, but the 'Active or Passive?' question should also be asked once the opening lead has been made and dummy tabled. Again, if the bidding, opening lead and dummy suggest that declarer is likely to make his contract, then desperate measures are called for; on the other hand, if dummy is minimum for his bidding, the opening lead has done no harm, and the defence's high cards seem to be sitting badly for declarer, all that is necessary is to give nothing away. Often the contract will make whatever you do, but the above strategy will not allow declarer to make anything he shouldn't.

Try it Yourself

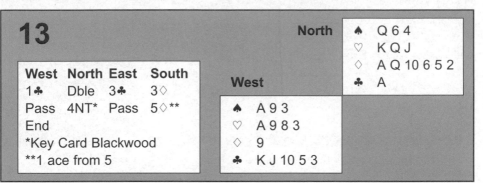

13

West	North	East	South
1♣	Dble	3♣	3◇
Pass	4NT*	Pass	5◇**
End			

*Key Card Blackwood
**1 ace from 5

North
♠ Q 6 4
♡ K Q J
◇ A Q 10 6 5 2
♣ A

West
♠ A 9 3
♡ A 9 8 3
◇ 9
♣ K J 10 5 3

You lead the ♣J and dummy's ace wins, partner playing the ♣4. Declarer plays a diamond to his king, partner following, and ruffs a club, partner playing the ♣8. Now he plays the ♡K, partner playing the ♡5 and declarer the ♡2. Plan the defence.

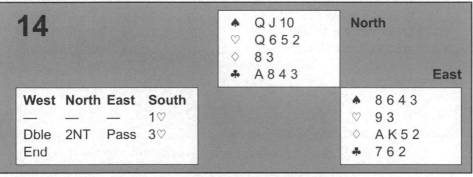

14

♠ Q J 10
♡ Q 6 5 2
◇ 8 3
♣ A 8 4 3

North

East
♠ 8 6 4 3
♡ 9 3
◇ A K 5 2
♣ 7 6 2

West	North	East	South
—	—	—	1♡
Dble	2NT	Pass	3♡
End			

West leads the ◇Q. Plan the defence.

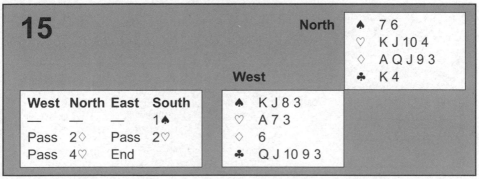

15

West	North	East	South
—	—	—	1♠
Pass	2◇	Pass	2♡
Pass	4♡	End	

North
♠ 7 6
♡ K J 10 4
◇ A Q J 9 3
♣ K 4

West
♠ K J 8 3
♡ A 7 3
◇ 6
♣ Q J 10 9 3

Reasoning that the spades and diamonds lie badly for declarer, you reject your solid club sequence in favour of leading a trump. Declarer wins in the dummy and plays a spade to his queen and your king, partner playing the ♠9. What now?

16

West	North	East	South
—	—	—	1NT*
Pass	2♣	Pass	2♡
Pass	3NT	End	
*15–17			

North
- ♠ Q 9 5 2
- ♡ 6
- ◇ A K J
- ♣ J 10 9 7 5

West
- ♠ A J 4
- ♡ Q 9 7 5 2
- ◇ 8 7 6
- ♣ Q 6

Despite knowing of declarer's four-card heart suit, you lead the ♡5 to partner's ♡J and declarer's ♡K. Declarer plays a diamond to dummy's king (partner playing the ◇2) and runs the ♣J to your queen (partner playing the ♣2).

17

♠ Q J 9 6
♡ Q 10 5 4
◇ A 5 3
♣ K 3

North

East
- ♠ A 3 2
- ♡ J 9 8 2
- ◇ J 10 8
- ♣ 8 7 4

West	North	East	South
—	—	—	1NT*
Pass	2♣	Pass	2♠
Pass	4♠	End	
*12–14			

Partner leads the ♣Q, which declarer wins with dummy's king, plays a club to his ace and ruffs a club (partner playing the ♣6 followed by the ♣5). He now plays the ♠Q from the dummy. Plan the defence.

18

♠ Q 5
♡ J 8
◇ 7 6 2
♣ K Q 10 9 4 2

North

East
- ♠ J 10 8 7
- ♡ Q 10 9 2
- ◇ K J 4
- ♣ A 6

West	North	East	South
—	—	—	1NT*
Pass	3NT	End	
*15–17			

West leads the ♡6. Declarer plays the ♡J from the dummy and wins your queen with his king. He now plays the ♣J which you duck and another club which you win, your partner playing the ♣8 followed by the ♣7. What now?

Solutions

13 Partner's play in clubs, along with his bidding, suggests a five-card suit there, and his ♡5 is certainly not from a four-card holding (it cannot be second highest). So there is no need to do anything active at all. Win, return a heart, and let declarer play spades himself. If you do this you must make two defensive tricks in spades, while if you broach the suit yourself you will make only one.

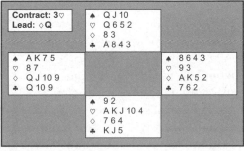

14 Partner's most likely distribution for his double is 4-2-4-3 (he would usually have four spades for a minimum double of 1♡; declarer would probably have bid 4♡ if he had had a six-card heart suit). If that is the case, declarer will be able to set up one or two spade tricks for a minor-suit discard. You need to switch to a club now. So, overtake the ◇Q with the ◇K and switch to the ♣7. When partner gets in with a spade he can play another diamond to your ace to get another club through.

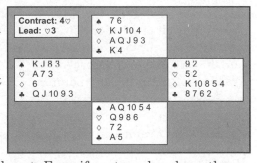

15 You should not let yourself be put off by dummy's good diamond suit. Your reasoning behind the original trump lead was sound. Stick with it! While it is just possible that partner has the ♣A and you could cash two tricks in the suit immediately, it is much more likely that declarer has it. Continue with the ♡A and another heart. Even if partner does have the ♣A and declarer has ◇K-x, declarer still has only nine tricks: one spade, two top trumps, a ruff in each hand, and four diamonds. For it to be wrong to play ace and another trump, declarer needs precisely ◇K-10 doubleton.

16 You know that declarer has the ♡A-K and may have the ♣A-K as well, though it is possible partner has a top club honour. It also looks as if declarer has a four-card diamond suit, quite likely headed by the queen. You are not going to beat 3NT on a passive defence. The only place where you

Contract: 3NT	♠ Q 9 5 2
Lead: ♡5	♡ 6
	◇ A K J
	♣ J 10 9 7 5

♠ A J 4		♠ K 10 7 6
♡ Q 9 7 5 2		♡ J 8 4
◇ 8 7 6		◇ 5 4 2
♣ Q 6		♣ 8 3 2

	♠ 8 3
	♡ A K 10 3
	◇ Q 10 9 3
	♣ A K 4

may be able to take enough tricks is in spades, and you must play partner to hold K-10-x-x. You should switch to the ♠J. Partner may be a little puzzled at first but either the ♠J will hold, in which case playing the ♠A and another will explain things to partner; alternatively declarer will cover with the ♠Q and when partner's king holds he should work out what to do.

17 You should play low on this spade trick, win the spade continuation and return a spade. You can tell from your red-suit holdings that there can be no benefit in attacking a red suit. Partner has shown you five clubs and there is a real danger that by switching to a red suit you will give

Contract: 4♠	♠ Q J 9 6
Lead: ♣Q	♡ Q 10 5 4
	◇ A 5 3
	♣ K 3

♠ 5 4		♠ A 3 2
♡ A 7 6		♡ J 9 8 2
◇ K 6 4		◇ J 10 8
♣ Q J 10 6 5		♣ 8 7 4

	♠ K 10 8 7
	♡ K 3
	◇ Q 9 7 2
	♣ A 9 2

declarer a trick there. On this layout, a switch to a heart would not affect the outcome, but a diamond switch would be fatal.

18 You should use the Rule of Eleven at trick one. Subtracting six from eleven leaves you with five, and you can see five cards higher than the six in dummy and your own hand. However, declarer played another at trick one. So partner cannot have led fourth highest and probably chose

Contract: 3NT	♠ Q 5
Lead: ♡6	♡ J 8
	◇ 7 6 2
	♣ K Q 10 9 4 2

♠ 6 4 2		♠ J 10 8 7
♡ 7 6 4 3		♡ Q 10 9 2
◇ A 10 5 3		◇ K J 4
♣ 8 7		♣ A 6

	♠ A K 9 3
	♡ A K 5
	◇ Q 9 8
	♣ J 5 3

second highest from a poor suit. If you do not take four tricks immediately, declarer will surely make his contract now dummy's clubs are established. Partner can have only between 4 and 6 high-card points, so his spades cannot be good enough and you must switch to a diamond; the ◇K followed by the ◇J will make it easy for partner (and stop declarer blocking the suit by going in with the queen at a suitable moment.

Chapter Four

Discarding

- **Counting the Hand**
- **Keeping Parity**
- **When to Ruff and when to Discard**
- **Avoiding the Endplay**

Discarding is one of the hardest aspects of defence, though some of the basic agreements regarding co-operative signalling can help. This chapter should help keep you on the right lines.

Counting the Hand

Discard from long weak suits, giving count to help partner build a picture of the hand.

There are many different legal methods of communicating with partner when you are discarding: 'revolving', 'suit preference', 'throw what you don't want', etc, etc. But what I would recommend is the simple count signal. While no method is perfect, in my experience, when you have a count of the hand you can usually work out what to do.

So, you play low with an odd number, and top of a doubleton or second highest from any other even number, just as if you were following to declarer's lead. As you will generally be discarding from weak suits, you can use your remaining spot cards to show suit preference.

Suppose that you are discarding from an original holding of 9-8-7-6. You first play the eight to show an even number. But if you continue with the seven followed by the six you show values in the higher-ranking suit, while if you play the six followed by the seven you prefer the lower-ranking suit, or you are neutral.

However, this chapter is more concerned with the general principles of discarding, rather than in promoting one particular type of signal.

Keeping Parity

This rather daunting phrase simply means that in general you should try to keep the same number of cards in a suit as you can see in dummy or know are in declarer's hand. This is particularly important when you have four cards in the same suit(s) as dummy.

Only when you are sure that your cards are so small as to be inconsequential should you voluntarily come down to fewer cards in the suit than dummy. Obviously if dummy has A-K-Q-J then your holding cannot possibly be relevant; equally, if dummy has K-9-8-7 and you have 6-4-3-2 then you can discard the suit. However, if dummy has A-K-J-7 and you have 8-5-4-2, then your eight may well be important (if partner has Q-10-9).

Here is an example:

> When discarding give priority to keeping the same number of cards as the hand sitting under you.

	North	
	♠ A Q 7 5	
	♡ A K 7 3	
	♢ A Q 7 5	
West	♣ 3	**East**
♠ J 10 9		♠ 8 6 4 2
♡ 10 9 8		♡ Q J 6 4
♢ 10 9 2		♢ 8 4
♣ J 10 6 5		♣ 9 8 7
	♠ K 3	
	♡ 5 2	
South	♢ K J 6 3	
	♣ A K Q 4 2	

South opened a 15–17 One No-trump and North used Stayman before asking for aces and kings and settling in Seven No-trumps. He would have done better to investigate for a diamond fit.

Declarer won the jack of spades lead in hand and played three rounds of clubs, discarding a diamond and a heart. He then played four rounds of diamonds and East had to find two discards. Helped by West's count signals (high-low in clubs and low-high in diamonds), East could work out that declarer must have four diamonds and five clubs, and because of his One No-trump opening had to be 2-2 in the majors. Therefore it was safe to throw two hearts. At the end, the eight of spades scored the thirteenth trick.

When to Ruff and when to Discard

This is a tricky topic which will be covered in more detail in later chapters, but good general advice is not to squander your trumps.

Don't ruff thin air

If declarer leads a low card towards an honour and you are void in the suit, it is rarely right to ruff. Quite often you are effectively ruffing partner's winner. Even if it looks as though your trump holding is inconsequential, it is surprising how those small trumps can be an inconvenience to declarer.

Don't ruff in unless you are sure you are ruffing one of declarer's tricks.

Only if you can see a certain route to defeating his contract should you ruff in in that position (and I will have a bet with you that you would have defeated the contract by at least as many tricks had you discarded instead!).

Overruff or discard?

When declarer ruffs and you can overruff, it is very tempting to do so, but it is not always right, as we will see later. There are three main reasons why it may work better for you not to do so:

(1)   You may promote a trump trick by failing to overruff. Suppose declarer began with K-Q-J-x-x-x and you had A-10-x. If you overruff when declarer ruffs high, you make only one trump trick; if instead you discard you have two trump tricks.

(2)   When you overruff you are effectively allowing declarer to use only one of his trumps to draw one of yours. Suppose, for example, he was in a 4-4 fit and you had the three-card defensive holding. If declarer cashes the ace and king and then goes about his business, if you overruff there will still be two trumps in the other hand for him to use for ruffing purposes. However, if you can gain the lead, you would be able to play a trump and draw two of his for one of yours.

(3)   Sometimes you may be able to discard from a suit in which you are also short, in order to get a more useful ruff later on.

Avoiding the Endplay

While this is a rather advanced subject for this book, you should try to project the play as far ahead as you can. If you have most of your side's defensive assets, you should consider discarding some of your high cards in order to avoid being endplayed later. Such a position might be if partner led a jack from J-10-x or J-10-x-x and you had the king and queen. It may well be better for you to discard the king and queen, retaining a small card so you can reach your partner's hand.

Try it Yourself

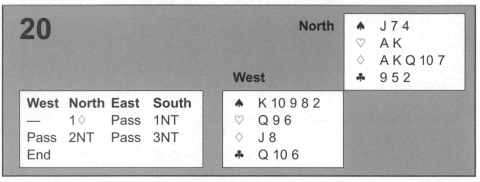

19

North
- ♠ A 7 5 4
- ♡ 8 5 3
- ◇ K 8
- ♣ A K 8 3

West
- ♠ Q 6 3
- ♡ A K J 9 2
- ◇ Q 9 7 6 3
- ♣ —

West	North	East	South
—	1♣	Pass	1♠
Dble	3♠	Pass	4♠
End			

You lead out ♡A-K-2, partner turning up with Q-7-6. Declarer ruffs and plays a spade to dummy's ace and a spade to his king, partner following twice. Then declarer plays a low club towards dummy. Over to you.

20

North
- ♠ J 7 4
- ♡ A K
- ◇ A K Q 10 7
- ♣ 9 5 2

West
- ♠ K 10 9 8 2
- ♡ Q 9 6
- ◇ J 8
- ♣ Q 10 6

West	North	East	South
—	1◇	Pass	1NT
Pass	2NT	Pass	3NT
End			

You lead the ♠10 to the four, three and ace. Declarer now proceeds to rattle off his five diamond tricks. What do you discard?

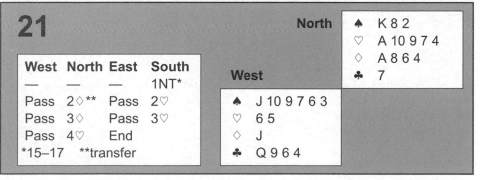

21

North
- ♠ K 8 2
- ♡ A 10 9 7 4
- ◇ A 8 6 4
- ♣ 7

West
- ♠ J 10 9 7 6 3
- ♡ 6 5
- ◇ J
- ♣ Q 9 6 4

West	North	East	South
—	—	—	1NT*
Pass	2◇**	Pass	2♡
Pass	3◇	Pass	3♡
Pass	4♡	End	
*15–17	**transfer		

You lead the ◇J against Four Hearts. Declarer wins in hand with the king, partner playing the ◇3. Declarer now runs the ♡Q to partner's king and partner continues with the ◇Q. Do you ruff or do you discard?

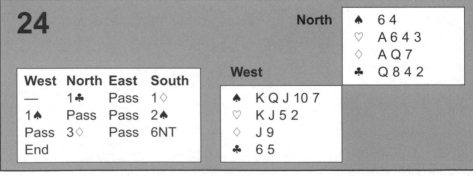

22

				North	♠ 6 5 3
					♡ J 5
					◇ Q 5 2
				West	♣ A J 10 6 5

West	North	East	South
—	—	2♠*	2NT
Pass	3NT	End	
*weak			

West hand:
♠ 2
♡ Q 9 8 7 2
◇ J 10 8 4 3
♣ K 3

You lead the ♠2, which partner wins with the ♠A and returns the ♠10. Declarer wins with the ♠K. What do you discard?

23

				North	♠ —
					♡ K 9 7 5 4
					◇ Q 10 8 3
				West	♣ Q 9 4 3

West	North	East	South
1NT*	Pass	Pass	2♠
End			
*12–14			

West hand:
♠ K 8 4 3 2
♡ Q J
◇ 9 7 5
♣ A K 6

For better or worse, as West you decide to lead the ♡Q. Declarer wins with the ace, partner playing the two. Declarer now plays the ♠A and ♠Q. You duck in order to get a signal from partner. Declarer continues with the ♠J, you win and partner discards the ◇2. Dummy meanwhile has discarded a card from each suit. Plan the defence.

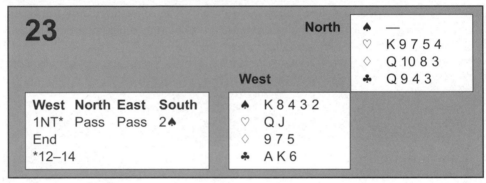

24

				North	♠ 6 4
					♡ A 6 4 3
					◇ A Q 7
				West	♣ Q 8 4 2

West	North	East	South
—	1♣	Pass	1◇
1♠	Pass	Pass	2♠
Pass	3◇	Pass	6NT
End			

West hand:
♠ K Q J 10 7
♡ K J 5 2
◇ J 9
♣ 6 5

Against South's slam you lead the ♠K on which partner plays the ♠8 and declarer wins the ♠A. Declarer proceeds to cash six (!) rounds of clubs (partner, who started with a singleton, first discards the ♠2, then the ♡7 and the ◇3). What is your discarding strategy?

Solutions

19 You must discard on this trick. You do not yet know declarer's club holding, but nothing can be gained by ruffing in at this stage with your trump winner. When you do decide to ruff in, make sure you are ruffing one of declarer's winners, not one of your own! Here, if you ruff the first club, you are effectively ruffing partner's winner.

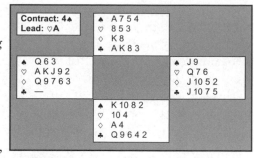

20 Count declarer's known winners. He has one spade trick, two hearts and five diamonds. If he has the ♣A as well, then he has nine tricks, so you must assume that your partner has the ♣A. You must be sure to hang on to all your spades. If declarer does not have the ♣A he has no entry to his hand, so it does not matter whether you discard hearts or clubs.

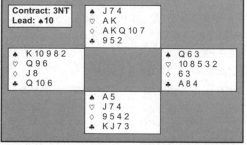

21 Even though your remaining trump is lowly and inconsequential, you should still not ruff in. Partner's play in diamonds marks him with a very strong holding in the suit. He is not leading it for you to ruff, he is leading it to knock out dummy's stopper in the suit. Then when he gets in with the ace of clubs he can cash two diamond tricks. If you make the mistake of ruffing the diamond, a good club guess by declarer will see him home.

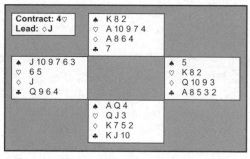

22 There is little room for partner to have a sure entry and a spade suit that is now established. With your ♣K looking well placed for declarer, the situation seems hopeless. But if your ♣K is useless you can afford to throw it away, and then if partner holds the ♣Q he may be able to gain the lead. So discard the ♣K.

Contract: 3NT	♠ 6 5 3	
Lead: ♠2	♥ J 5	
	♦ Q 5 2	
	♣ A J 10 6 5	
♠ 2		♠ A Q J 10 8 4
♥ Q 9 8 7 2		♥ 10 4 3
♦ J 10 8 4 3		♦ 7 6
♣ K 3		♣ Q 2
	♠ K 9 7	
	♥ A K 6	
	♦ A K 9	
	♣ 9 8 7 4	

23 It looks likely that your partner has the ♦A-K, because declarer has already shown up with quite a lot and may well have preferred to double 1NT had he had another high card. If partner had started with five hearts he would probably not have passed 1NT, so you must play him

Contract: 2♠	♠ —	
Lead: ♥Q	♥ K 9 7 5 4	
	♦ Q 10 8 3	
	♣ Q 9 4 3	
♠ K 8 4 3 2		♠ 6 5
♥ Q J		♥ 10 3 2
♦ 9 7 5		♦ A K 6 4 2
♣ A K 6		♣ 8 7 2
	♠ A Q J 10 9 7	
	♥ A 8 6	
	♦ J	
	♣ J 10 5	

for ♥10-x-x. Return another heart, which will leave declarer stranded in the dummy. In this type of position partner should always discard from his five-card suit, so he has told you how to defend. When declarer comes off dummy with a club, you win with the ♣K, cash the ♣A and play a diamond. Partner will win the diamond, cash the ♥10 on which you will discard a club, and now a club ruff will beat the contract.

24 Assuming declarer has the ♦K, you can count eleven tricks for him: one spade, one heart, three diamonds (if he has four diamond tricks you have no chance) and six clubs. His only chance of a twelfth trick is to throw you in with a spade to lead hearts for him. There is no use your

Contract: 6NT	♠ 6 4	
Lead: ♠K	♥ A 6 4 3	
	♦ A Q 7	
	♣ Q 8 4 2	
♠ K Q J 10 7		♠ 9 8 3 2
♥ K J 5 2		♥ 10 9 7
♦ J 9		♦ 10 8 6 5 3
♣ 6 5		♣ 3
	♠ A 5	
	♥ Q 8	
	♦ K 4 2	
	♣ A K J 10 9 7	

blanking your ♥K for he will surely read the position, given your 1♠ overcall. But partner's ♠8 at trick one and subsequent discard of the ♠2 does suggest he started with a spade holding of 9-8-x-x. If this is the case you can discard all your top spades, leaving it to partner to keep the suit. Then when he gets in with the ♠9 he can either cash a good spade or lead a heart through declarer.

Chapter Five

More on Signalling

- **Giving Count when Playing the Suit Led**
- **More on Suit Preference**
- **Suit Preference in Trumps**

We looked at basic signalling in *Chapter One*, but as you get more experienced you can take more on board. In this chapter we are going to look at more ways to tell partner about your hand.

Giving Count when Playing the Suit Led

In *Chapter One* we saw that there are conventions concerning which card to return in partner's suit. There are similar agreements when following or discarding in the suit partner has led.

$\heartsuit$ 8 7

$\heartsuit$ A 10 6 5 2 $\heartsuit$ Q 9 4

$\heartsuit$ K J 3

Suppose partner leads the five of hearts against a no-trump contract. You play the queen and declarer wins with the king. He now rattles off some long suit and you want to discard a heart. Which heart should you discard? The answer is that you should discard the same card that you would have returned, i.e. the nine.

Similarly, were partner to get the lead and cash the ace of this suit, again you should play the nine, the same card that you would have returned. This system of showing count is often called 'giving present count' and, indeed, may be an easier way for you to look at it. You pretend that you never had the top honour you have already played and play accordingly, i.e. high-low from a doubleton, and low from three.

> MUD is a signalling method to indicate to partner your length in a weak suit.

Here is a different situation. Suppose you decide to lead the seven of clubs from one of the following holdings:

9 7 4   9 7 4 2   9 7 4 3 2

Which card are you going to play the next time the suit is played?

From the three-card holding you should next play upwards, i.e. the nine. The reason you led the seven in the first place was because you play MUD, Middle Up Down.

From the four-card holding, you should play the two, your original fourth highest.

From the five-card holding I would recommend you play the four (though some would argue for the nine on the grounds that it makes it clearer that you have an odd number and partner will usually be able to tell the difference between three and five).

More on Suit Preference

Suit preference when following with small cards

As we saw in the previous chapter when we looked at discarding, even though your primary method of signalling when following suit or discarding may be 'count', there are numerous opportunities to help partner further with carefully selected cards.

Suppose that your holding in the first suit declarer plays is 8-6-4. The first card you play is the four to show an odd number, but on the second round you have a free choice between the eight and the six. The one you choose should depend on your suit preference.

Now all you need is a partner who notices!

Suit preference with honours

> You can use the order in which you play your honour cards to tell partner more about your hand.

Sometimes it is not possible to give a suit-preference signal with your small cards, so you have to do it with your honours. Suppose this is the layout of a side-suit is a suit contract:

```
                 J 10 6
      9 8      [            ]      A K Q 7 5 4
                 3 2
```

Partner leads the nine and it is your intention to play your three top honours, hoping to promote a trump trick in your partner's hand. You could play your three honours in any order. The way to show strength in the higher-ranking suit would be to play ace, king, queen, while the way to show strength in the lower suit would be queen, king, ace.

Showing ace-king doubleton

The normal lead from ace-king in most parts of the world is the ace. If a king is led followed by the ace it generally shows ace-king doubleton. So, when partner leads the king followed by the ace he wants you to tell him how to put you in, and your second card should be a suit-preference signal.

When there is a singleton in dummy

Against a suit contract, when partner leads a high honour that will probably win the trick and there is a singleton in dummy, there is usually not a lot of point in showing attitude or giving count. Most often he would be more interested in knowing what suit you would like him to switch to. Again, a high card calls for the higher-ranking suit, while a low card calls for the lower-ranking suit. A middle card would suggest either a trump switch, or a continuation of the suit led.

When declarer has a singleton

A variation on the above is when you know that declarer has a singleton. Say you and your partner have supported hearts so are known to have at least an eight-card fit in the suit. When partner leads a top heart against an opposing spade contract, say, and dummy comes down with four hearts, you both know that by the end of this trick declarer will have no more cards in the suit. Again, this is a good moment for a suit-preference signal.

Signalling in Trumps

The traditional meaning of a high-low signal in trumps is to indicate the desire to ruff. Suppose you lead a singleton which is won by declarer, who then plays a trump which your partner wins with the ace. You play a high trump to tell partner that your lead was a singleton.

However, as with everything else, fashions change. These days many pairs prefer to play a peter in trumps as either giving count – on some hands it is very important to know how good a fit declarer has – or suit preference.

Try it Yourself

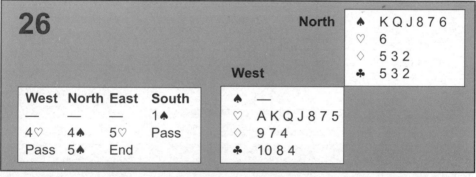

25

	♠ K Q 10 8	North
	♡ 6	
	◇ 7 6 3	
	♣ A Q J 7 4	East

West	North	East	South
2◇*	3♣	Pass	3♡
Pass	3♠	Pass	3NT
End			
*weak			

East:
♠ 6 5 3 2
♡ 9 8 5 3
◇ 9 2
♣ K 6 5

West leads the ◇K, on which declarer plays the ◇J. Partner continues with the ◇Q, won by declarer's ace. Declarer next plays the ♣10 which you win with the king. What now?

26

North:
♠ K Q J 8 7 6
♡ 6
◇ 5 3 2
♣ 5 3 2

West:
♠ —
♡ A K Q J 8 7 5
◇ 9 7 4
♣ 10 8 4

West	North	East	South
—	—	—	1♠
4♡	4♠	5♡	Pass
Pass	5♠	End	

You lead the ♡A and partner plays the ten. What now?

27

North:
♠ K J 10 5
♡ 6
◇ Q 9 7 6 4
♣ A J 4

West:
♠ A 6 4 2
♡ 10 8 2
◇ 8
♣ K Q 10 7 3

West	North	East	South
—	—	—	1◇
Pass	1♠	Pass	2♡
Pass	4◇	Pass	4♡*
Pass	4NT*	Pass	5♣*
Pass	6◇	End	

South's 4♡ was a cue-bid, and North's 4NT Roman Key Card Blackwood, the 5♣ response showing 0 or 3 of the 5 aces (the ◇K counts as an ace). You lead the ♣K. Declarer wins with dummy's ace, East playing the ♣8. Declarer now plays a diamond to his ace and a low spade. Do you play high or low?

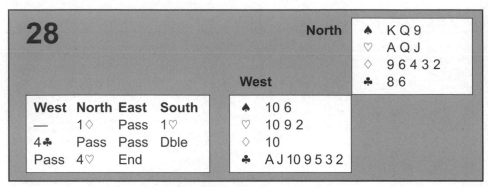

28

West	North	East	South
—	1◇	Pass	1♡
4♣	Pass	Pass	Dble
Pass	4♡	End	

North
♠ K Q 9
♡ A Q J
◇ 9 6 4 3 2
♣ 8 6

West
♠ 10 6
♡ 10 9 2
◇ 10
♣ A J 10 9 5 3 2

You lead the ◇10 which, rather unexpectedly, holds the trick, partner playing the ◇5 and declarer the ◇7. What now?

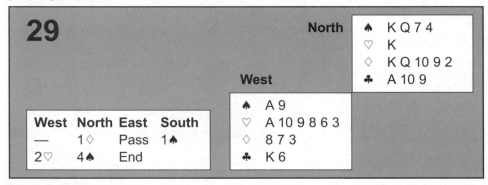

29

West	North	East	South
—	1◇	Pass	1♠
2♡	4♠	End	

North
♠ K Q 7 4
♡ K
◇ K Q 10 9 2
♣ A 10 9

West
♠ A 9
♡ A 10 9 8 6 3
◇ 8 7 3
♣ K 6

You lead the ♡A and partner plays the ♡2. What do you do at trick two?

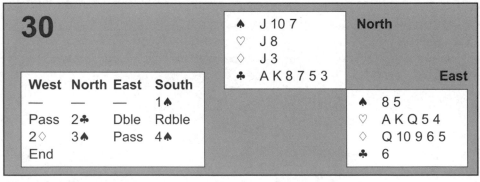

30

West	North	East	South
—	—	—	1♠
Pass	2♣	Dble	Rdble
2◇	3♠	Pass	4♠
End			

North
♠ J 10 7
♡ J 8
◇ J 3
♣ A K 8 7 5 3

East
♠ 8 5
♡ A K Q 5 4
◇ Q 10 9 6 5
♣ 6

Partner leads the ♡2 against 4♠. You win the ♡Q and continue with the ♡A, partner playing the ♡3. What do you do now?

Solutions

25 You should switch to a spade. When declarer's ◇J was played at trick one, the complete diamond distribution was an open book. Partner had a choice of five remaining diamonds to play to trick two and he chose the queen, his highest. He must have the ♠A.

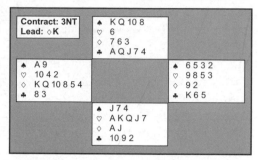

```
Contract: 3NT    ♠ K Q 10 8
Lead: ◇K         ♡ 6
                 ◇ 7 6 3
                 ♣ A Q J 7 4
♠ A 9                          ♠ 6 5 3 2
♡ 10 4 2                       ♡ 9 8 5 3
◇ K Q 10 8 5 4                 ◇ 9 2
♣ 8 3                          ♣ K 6 5
                 ♠ J 7 4
                 ♡ A K Q J 7
                 ◇ A J
                 ♣ 10 9 2
```

26 You should switch to a diamond. When there is a singleton in the dummy partner should give you suit preference rather than count or attitude. So, his ♡10 should be asking for a diamond. As you can see from the full deal, if you do anything else, declarer will make his contract.

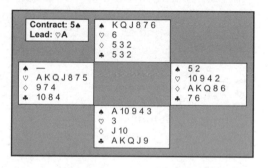

```
Contract: 5♠    ♠ K Q J 8 7 6
Lead: ♡A        ♡ 6
                ◇ 5 3 2
                ♣ 5 3 2
♠ —                            ♠ 5 2
♡ A K Q J 8 7 5                ♡ 10 9 4 2
◇ 9 7 4                        ◇ A K Q 8 6
♣ 10 8 4                       ♣ 7 6
                ♠ A 10 9 4 3
                ♡ 3
                ◇ J 10
                ♣ A K Q J 9
```

27 Normally when partner leads a king, you should tell him whether or not you like the suit. However, sometimes dummy's holding makes it obvious that you cannot like the suit, in which case you should give count instead. So partner's ♣8 was telling you that he had an even number – surely

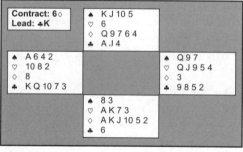

```
Contract: 6◇    ♠ K J 10 5
Lead: ♣K        ♡ 6
                ◇ Q 9 7 6 4
                ♣ A J 4
♠ A 6 4 2                      ♠ Q 9 7
♡ 10 8 2                       ♡ Q J 9 5 4
◇ 8                            ◇ 3
♣ K Q 10 7 3                   ♣ 9 8 5 2
                ♠ 8 3
                ♡ A K 7 3
                ◇ A K J 10 5 2
                ♣ 6
```

four on this occasion. So declarer has a singleton club and your only hope is that he misguesses spades. He has probably played the suit so early to put you under pressure, so it is no good dithering. You must play small smoothly.

28 Your opponents clearly had a misunderstanding about the nature of South's double. When your partner leaves you on lead at trick one with the ◇10, and plays his lowest card in the suit, he is surely asking you to play a club. And he would only do that if he had a void club or the king – if he had a singleton or the queen he would have overtaken the diamond and played a club through declarer. It is important that you switch to a *low* club. Partner will ruff and play another diamond which declarer will ruff high. Declarer can draw trumps and enjoy his spades, but can come to only one club trick and so make nine in total. If you make the mistake of cashing the ♣A at trick two, he will make his contract.

29 Switch to the ♣K. Partner's ♡2, with a singleton in dummy, is a suit-preference signal for the lowest suit. When you switch to the ♣K, declarer has no winning line of play. If he wins you can get a club ruff when you win the ♠A, while if he ducks your partner has a second natural club winner.

30 Partner has clearly led a heart from either 10-3-2 or 9-3-2. On the second round his choice of card should be influenced by his suit preference. He is trying to tell you that there is no future in the diamond suit. Therefore you switch to your singleton club. Although partner has nothing in clubs, when he gets the lead with the ♠A he gives you a club ruff.

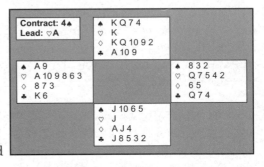

Chapter Six

More on Second and Third Hand Play

- **When Second Hand Should Play High**
- **Cover an Honour with an Honour**
- **When Third Hand Should Play Low**

In *Chapter Two*, we looked at some general rules, in particular 'Second Hand Low' and 'Third Hand High'. It probably will come as no surprise to hear that there are plenty of exceptions to those rules and that is what we will look at in this chapter.

Also another good piece of general advice, 'Cover an honour with an honour', is looked at, and of course there are exceptions to that exhortation as well.

When Second Hand Should Play High

When partner is the player with the established tricks, do what you can to preserve his entries.

There are two main reasons for a defender who is second in hand to play a high card.

Preserving partner's entries
Suppose two suits are dealt like this:

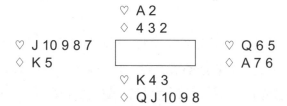

♡ A 2
◇ 4 3 2

♡ J 10 9 8 7   ♡ Q 6 5
◇ K 5   ◇ A 7 6

♡ K 4 3
◇ Q J 10 9 8

Partner leads the ♡J against a no-trump contract. Declarer ducks and wins the second round in the dummy to play a diamond. If you, East, play low, partner's entry will disappear before he needs it, but if you rise with the ◇A, you can clear the hearts while partner still has the ◇K as an entry.

Preventing declarer from ducking the trick
When a loser in a suit is inevitable, declarer's communication problems are often eased if he can duck an early round of the suit. If you are the 'danger hand' you can sometimes stop him doing this by inserting a high card.

Cover an Honour with an Honour

This is a well-known adage, but is it valid? As is the case with most such advice, it is true more often than not, but there are some exceptions.

There are two different types of simple finesse position:

(1)   A J x   (2)   A x x

      Q x x   Q J x

In the first layout, it is very important, should you hold the king as West, for you to cover when declarer leads the queen from hand. If you play low, the queen will hold and declarer will take another finesse on the next round, thus making three tricks when he was entitled to only two.

On the other layout, however, it does not really matter whether you cover the queen, or whether you wait and cover the jack on the next round. Either way declarer will make two tricks and two tricks only.

Try another layout:

(3)   A x x

      Q J 9

<table>
<tr><td>Cover the
last of
touching
honours.</td></tr>
</table>

Now if you cover the queen, declarer will be in dummy with a finesse position against partner's ten, should he hold it. By covering on the first round you may have allowed declarer to make three tricks when he was entitled to only two.

If declarer's first play is from the dummy the position is fairly straightforward. You wait until declarer plays the last honour from dummy before covering.

So, if he leads the queen from Q-x-x, you cover straight away if you hold the king. If he has Q-J-x in the dummy, you wait until the second round before you cover. And if he has Q-J-10, then there is nothing to be gained by covering before the third round.

In addition to all this, you should never cover if you hold more cards in the suit than the hand with the ace.

Consider this layout:

(4)   Q J 10 9 8
          x   [_____] K x x x
                      A x x

By covering the honour at any stage you lose your trick in this suit. This situation can be quite hard to see; I recently saw somebody let through a grand slam by covering in this position.

When Third Hand Should Play Low

While the principle of playing high in third seat to force declarer to play a high card is sound, when the highest card you hold is likely to be completely ineffectual, you are better to give partner count. For example, suppose this is the layout:

K 6 4

2 led   8 7 3

What could partner have? If he had three honours he would surely have led one, so he is going to have something like: A-J-9-2, A-J-5-2 or Q-10-5-2. If partner has the five it can never cost for you to play your three; and even if declarer has the five and wins the trick with it, he has not made more tricks than were his by right. Meanwhile, by playing the three you tell partner clearly that you have a three-card holding, whereas if you played the seven he might think you had 7-3 doubleton or 8-7-x-x.

Be careful not to play a high card when it sets up tricks in dummy.

Another situation when it is right for third hand to play low is in order to avoid giving declarer too many tricks. Consider a couple of layouts:

(1)	Q 10 9		(2)	J 10 2	
J 7 6 2		K 8 5	A 8 7 5 4		Q 6 3
	A 4 3			K 9	

On the first layout, partner leads the two. If you play the king when declarer plays the ten from dummy, you will allow him to make three tricks in the suit. If you play low he can make only two – though, admittedly, you will not be able to play the suit again, and there are all sorts of potential dangers lying ahead for you because both of you will need to keep two cards in the suit, but at least you have not presented him with that extra trick too easily.

On the second layout partner leads the five and dummy plays the jack. If you play the queen, declarer will have two tricks in the suit, while if you manage to duck this, declarer has only one trick. Again, it may be difficult for you to untangle this suit. On the next round you need to play low to partner's ace, which will block the suit, so he will need to be able to gain the lead again in order to cash out. But at least it gives you a chance.

Try it Yourself

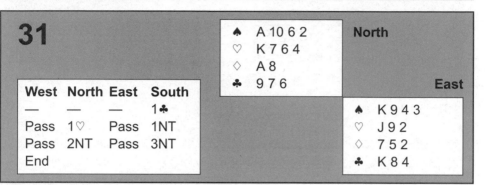

31

West	North	East	South
—	—	—	1♣
Pass	1♡	Pass	1NT
Pass	2NT	Pass	3NT
End			

North
♠ A 10 6 2
♡ K 7 6 4
◇ A 8
♣ 9 7 6

East
♠ K 9 4 3
♡ J 9 2
◇ 7 5 2
♣ K 8 4

West leads the ◇Q, which holds, followed by the ◇3, which is won by dummy's ace. Declarer plays the ♣6 from the dummy. Plan the defence.

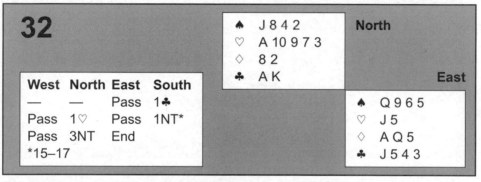

32

West	North	East	South
—	—	Pass	1♣
Pass	1♡	Pass	1NT*
Pass	3NT	End	
*15–17			

North
♠ J 8 4 2
♡ A 10 9 7 3
◇ 8 2
♣ A K

East
♠ Q 9 6 5
♡ J 5
◇ A Q 5
♣ J 5 4 3

West leads the ◇4. Plan the defence.

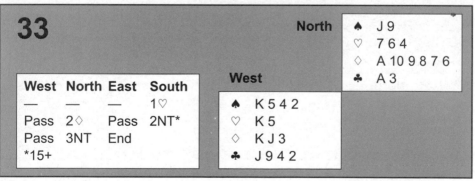

33

West	North	East	South
—	—	—	1♡
Pass	2◇	Pass	2NT*
Pass	3NT	End	
*15+			

North
♠ J 9
♡ 7 6 4
◇ A 10 9 8 7 6
♣ A 3

West
♠ K 5 4 2
♡ K 5
◇ K J 3
♣ J 9 4 2

You lead the ♠2 to the ♠J, ♠Q and declarer's ace. At trick two declarer plays the ◇Q. How do you defend?

34

		♠	A J 10 8 5	**North**
		♡	A 6	
		◇	Q J 4	
		♣	10 8 6	**East**

West	North	East	South
—	—	1NT*	Pass
Pass	2♡**	Pass	2♠
Dble	All Pass		
*10–12	**showing spades		

East
♠ Q 3 2
♡ 10 7 4
◇ K 9 5 3
♣ K Q 3

Partner leads the ♠4 and declarer plays dummy's jack. Plan the defence. Can you justify your decision to pass partner's double (which usually shows a doubleton spade)?

35

		♠	7 6 2	**North**
		♡	K Q 7 6	
		◇	9 5 3	
		♣	Q 10 9	**East**

West	North	East	South
—	—	—	2NT
Pass	3♣	Pass	3♡
Pass	4♡	End	

East
♠ Q 10 9 3
♡ 9 3 2
◇ 8 4 2
♣ K 7 5

West leads the ♣3. Declarer plays the ♣10 from dummy. Plan the defence.

36

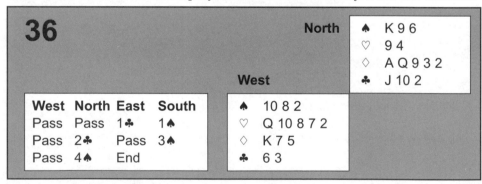

North
♠ K 9 6
♡ 9 4
◇ A Q 9 3 2
♣ J 10 2

West
♠ 10 8 2
♡ Q 10 8 7 2
◇ K 7 5
♣ 6 3

West	North	East	South
Pass	Pass	1♣	1♠
Pass	2♣	Pass	3♠
Pass	4♠	End	

At trick one you lead the ♣6, covered by dummy ten, partner's queen and declarer's ace. Declarer draws three rounds of trumps (East following twice) and then leads the ◇6 from hand. How are you going to defend?

Solutions

31 If you play a low club, declarer will play the ♣Q and partner will win his ace (it will not help him to duck). He will now be able to knock out declarer's remaining diamond stopper but he will have no entry with which to gain the lead in order to cash his diamonds. You must rise with your

Contract: 3NT	♠ A 10 6 2	
Lead: ◇Q	♡ K 7 6 4	
	◇ A 8	
	♣ 9 7 6	
♠ Q 7 5		♠ K 9 4 3
♡ 8 5 3		♡ J 9 2
◇ Q J 10 9 3		◇ 7 5 2
♣ A 5		♣ K 8 4
	♠ J 8	
	♡ A Q 10	
	◇ K 6 4	
	♣ Q J 10 3 2	

♣K to protect his entry. When the ♣K holds, you play another diamond. Declarer will win his king and play another club. Now when your partner wins his ace he will have two more diamond winners to cash. If declarer had had the ♣A-Q nothing would have been lost because your ♣K would have been doomed in any event.

32 If you win the ◇A at trick one and return the ◇Q, of course you will be all right if partner started with ◇K-x-x-x-x, but suppose declarer has the ◇K. He will duck until the third round and when you gain the lead in clubs you will not have another diamond to play. Instead you

Contract: 3NT	♠ J 8 4 2	
Lead: ◇4	♡ A 10 9 7 3	
	◇ 8 2	
	♣ A K	
♠ 10 7 3		♠ Q 9 6 5
♡ Q 8 4 2		♡ J 5
◇ J 9 7 4 3		◇ A Q 5
♣ 6		♣ J 5 4 3
	♠ A K	
	♡ K 6	
	◇ K 10 6	
	♣ Q 10 9 8 7 2	

should play the ◇Q at trick one. As the cards lie declarer could still duck, but he cannot see through the back of the cards. He would look very silly if West held ◇A-J-x-x-x and clubs broke 3-2. He will surely win the ◇K, and then when you get in with the ♣J you can play the ◇A and a diamond to your partner's hand.

33 You must duck the ◇Q. You know that if you cover, declarer will win with dummy's ◇A and knock out your ◇J. Then with the ♣A as entry he can run the diamonds and will surely have enough tricks. You must hope that his ◇Q is singleton. Now by ducking you cut him off from all his diamond winners and he must go down.

Contract: 3NT	♠ J 9	
Lead: ♠2	♡ 7 6 4	
	◇ A 10 9 8 7 6	
	♣ A 3	
♠ K 5 4 2		♠ Q 10 8
♡ K 5		♡ 10 9 8 3
◇ K J 3		◇ 5 4 2
♣ J 9 4 2		♣ 8 7 6
	♠ A 7 6 3	
	♡ A Q J 2	
	◇ Q	
	♣ K Q 10 5	

34 This was a tight matchpointed pairs double of vulnerable opponents and you have to defend well to justify your decision to defend. It looks as if declarer has the ♠K, in which case it would be a mistake to play the ♠Q at trick one. If you do, declarer can win and play the ♡A and

Contract: 2♠ doubled Lead: ♠4		
	♠ A J 10 8 5 ♡ A 6 ◊ Q J 4 ♣ 10 8 6	
♠ 7 4 ♡ K Q 5 ◊ A 10 8 7 6 ♣ A 5 2		♠ Q 3 2 ♡ 10 7 4 ◊ K 9 5 3 ♣ K Q 3
	♠ K 9 6 ♡ J 9 8 3 2 ◊ 2 ♣ J 9 7 4	

another heart. He has two more trump entries to hand to set up and cash the hearts. However, look at what happens if you withhold your ♠Q at trick one. Declarer is an entry short to establish hearts, and if he tries to ruff two diamonds in hand he will promote a trick for your ♠Q.

35 It is important that you do not play your ♣K at trick one. You know that declarer has the ♣A, for partner would surely not underlead an ace with a 2NT opener on his right. If you play the ♣K, declarer will win his ace and later make two more club tricks by finessing partner's ♣J. If you

Contract: 4♡ Lead: ♣3		
	♠ 7 6 2 ♡ K Q 7 6 ◊ 9 5 3 ♣ Q 10 9	
♠ J 8 ♡ 8 5 ◊ A Q 10 7 ♣ J 6 4 3 2		♠ Q 10 9 3 ♡ 9 3 2 ◊ 8 4 2 ♣ K 7 5
	♠ A K 5 4 ♡ A J 10 4 ◊ K J 6 ♣ A 8	

withhold your ♣K you restrict declarer's winners to two and when all the diamonds are wrong and spades do not break he will have to go down.

36 If you play low on the diamond, declarer will play dummy's ◊9. The best your partner can do is put him to a heart guess, but, in the light of East's opening bid, declarer will surely rise with the ♡K. Then a diamond finesse will see the suit come in for plenty of tricks. But if you play the ◊K he

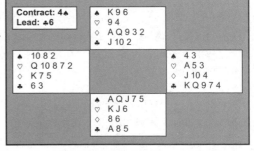

is doomed. If he ducks you can play a second club and take two tricks in that suit, while if he wins he is cut off from dummy's diamonds.

Chapter Seven

More on Active or Passive?

- **Should You Play Trumps?**
- **Neutralising Dummy's Long Suit**
- **The Switch Defence**

It may seem that I am belabouring a point to have another chapter on when to be active and when to be passive, but this so often seems to be where average players go wrong in defence. They switch blindly from one suit to another in a desperate attempt to find partner's high cards. On average, every time they switch they give away half a trick and the net result is that a contract is allowed to make that had no chance if declarer were left to his own devices.

Should You Play Trumps?

Generally speaking, you should lead or play trumps when your cards are situated badly for declarer. When you think he will have difficulty in establishing suits, then play trumps to stop him ruffing. However, when everything is breaking well you need to be more active and play on your best side-suit.

Here is an example:

	North
♠ 9 6	
♡ J	
◇ A Q 9 8 5 4	
♣ A 7 6 3	

West		East
♠ Q 4 2		♠ 5 3
♡ K Q 10 6		♡ A 9 5 3 2
◇ 6 2		◇ K J 10 3
♣ Q 9 8 5		♣ 10 2

	South
♠ A K J 10 8 7	
♡ 8 7 4	
◇ 7	
♣ K J 4	

> When side-suits are lying badly for declarer it is often right for the defenders to lead trumps.

South opened the bidding with One Spade, and rebid the suit both over North's Two Diamonds and his subsequent Three Clubs. North then raised to Four Spades.

West led the king of hearts and East had read the section in *Chapter Five* on giving suit preference when there is a singleton in dummy. So he played the nine of hearts, asking West to switch to a diamond. West duly obliged but declarer could now ruff two hearts in the dummy, eventually losing just one spade, one heart and one club.

East should have realised that there was no hurry to get a diamond switch. There was a much more pressing matter, that of trying to prevent heart ruffs in the dummy. East should further see that a trump switch is likely to be much more effective from his side. He should have overtaken the king of hearts with the ace and switched to a trump. Now declarer must lose two hearts, as well as a trump and a club.

Neutralising Dummy's Long Suit

Every now and then you find yourself defending against a suit contract where dummy has a strong side-suit. It is tempting to try to set up winners in the remaining two suits but, while this may be the winning defence, it can often work better to play dummy's suit early in the play. If dummy has no outside entries and you can exhaust declarer of his cards in the suit, then dummy will be dead.

Here is an example:

> When dummy has few entries and a long, good suit, consider switching to that suit to prevent declarer enjoying it later in the hand.

	North	
♠ J 6		
♡ A 6		
◊ K Q J 10 6		
♣ 10 6 5 3		

West

| ♠ K 7 4 |
| ♡ K Q J 2 |
| ◊ 5 3 |
| ♣ Q 9 8 4 |

East

| ♠ A 8 |
| ♡ 10 9 5 4 3 |
| ◊ 9 8 7 4 |
| ♣ K 7 |

South

| ♠ Q 10 9 5 3 2 |
| ♡ 8 7 |
| ◊ A 2 |
| ♣ A J 2 |

After the bidding sequence: 1♠ – 2◊ – 2♠ – 3♠ – end, West led the king of hearts. Declarer won with the ace (East playing the three) and played the jack of spades from the dummy. East went in with the ace and played a heart to West's jack. West knew that declarer did not need to ruff a heart in the dummy (because East surely had five). As long as declarer had only a doubleton diamond, it had to be right for the defenders to play that suit. So he switched to a diamond. Declarer won the ace and played another spade. West won his king and continued diamonds. Now was decision time for declarer. Should he continue with diamonds, hoping that they were 3-3 or that the hand with the doubleton diamond no longer had any trumps, or should he abandon diamonds and play clubs himself? the event he played a third diamond, discarding a club. West ruffed and declarer still had to lose a club trick for one down.

The Switch Defence

Having exhorted you to defend passively rather more often and issued dire warnings about frantically switching from one suit to another, I shall now look at a situation when such a busy defence is necessary.

Look at this example:

<table>
<tr><td rowspan="7">If you can see that declarer will succeed if you continue your suit, you must try something else.</td></tr>
</table>

	North
♠ 7 6	
♡ A 10 3	
◇ J 10 2	
♣ K Q J 10 5	

West		East	
♠ K Q 10 4 2		♠ 9 8 3	
♡ 9 8 6		♡ K Q 7 4	
◇ 8 7 3		◇ 9 6 4	
♣ 9 8		♣ A 3 2	

	South
♠ A J 5	
♡ J 5 2	
◇ A K Q 5	
♣ 7 6 4	

North/South bid 1NT – 3NT, and West leads the king of spades. South has to duck this trick, so West switches to the eight of hearts. If declarer wins this trick he will lose one spade, three hearts and a club, so he ducks again. East wins the queen and switches back to spades. Declarer still cannot afford to win, so he ducks again, and again West switches back to hearts. Declarer is doomed and must lose three hearts, two spades and a club. By winning the first trick in either major he could have settled for down one but could never make his contract.

Try it Yourself

37

West	North	East	South
—	—	—	1♣
Pass	1♥	Pass	2♠
Pass	3♥	Pass	4♥
Pass	5♦	Pass	6♣
End			

North
♠ 6 3
♥ A J 10 8 5 2
♦ A J 2
♣ 6 5

East
♠ K 4
♥ Q 9 4
♦ K Q 7 6 3
♣ 9 8 7

West leads the ♦4, declarer plays low from dummy and your ♦Q wins the first trick. Plan the defence.

38

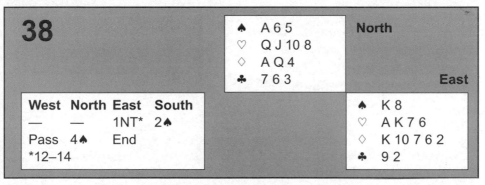

North
♠ A 6 5
♥ Q J 10 8
♦ A Q 4
♣ 7 6 3

East
♠ K 8
♥ A K 7 6
♦ K 10 7 6 2
♣ 9 2

West	North	East	South
—	—	1NT*	2♠
Pass	4♠	End	
*12–14			

Your slightly off-centre 1NT opening backfires when the opponents bid 4♠ and partner leads the ♣Q. Declarer wins with the ♣K and plays a spade to his ace and a second spade. Plan the defence.

39

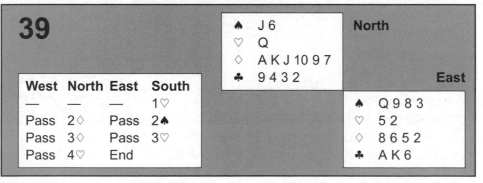

North
♠ J 6
♥ Q
♦ A K J 10 9 7
♣ 9 4 3 2

East
♠ Q 9 8 3
♥ 5 2
♦ 8 6 5 2
♣ A K 6

West	North	East	South
—	—	—	1♥
Pass	2♦	Pass	2♠
Pass	3♦	Pass	3♥
Pass	4♥	End	

Partner leads the ♣5. You cash the ♣A and ♣K, declarer following with the ♣8 and ♣J. What now?

40

West	North	East	South
Pass	Pass	Pass	1NT*
End			
*12–14			

North
♠ K 5
♥ 8 7 5
♦ K Q 10 8 7 2
♣ 8 3

West
♠ J 10 9 6
♥ A 6 4
♦ 9 6 3
♣ A Q 2

You lead the ♠J, covered by the king and partner's ace. Partner continues with the ♠Q and another spade (declarer started with four). On the fourth round of spades partner discards the ♣4. What do you do now?

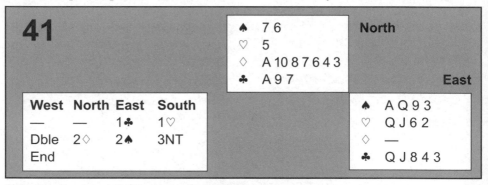

41

West	North	East	South
—	—	1♣	1♥
Dble	2♦	2♠	3NT
End			

North
♠ 7 6
♥ 5
♦ A 10 8 7 6 4 3
♣ A 9 7

East
♠ A Q 9 3
♥ Q J 6 2
♦ —
♣ Q J 8 4 3

West leads the ♠J. Plan the defence.

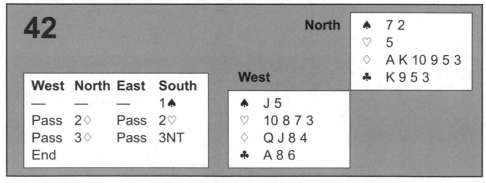

42

West	North	East	South
—	—	—	1♠
Pass	2♦	Pass	2♥
Pass	3♦	Pass	3NT
End			

North
♠ 7 2
♥ 5
♦ A K 10 9 5 3
♣ K 9 5 3

West
♠ J 5
♥ 10 8 7 3
♦ Q J 8 4
♣ A 8 6

You lead the ♥3 against South's 3NT, and partner's ♥K is headed by declarer's ace. Declarer next plays a low diamond to dummy's ten. He continues with the ◇A and another diamond (declarer started with a singleton). How do you defend?

Solutions

37 A heart switch looks out of the question, but a black-suit return seems unlikely to succeed either. Surely declarer will just win, draw trumps, ruff out the ♡Q and cross to dummy with the ◊A to run all the hearts. The only defence to stand a chance is to return a diamond – if declarer started with a

Contract: 6♣ Lead: ◊4	♠ 6 3 ♡ A J 10 8 5 2 ◊ A J 2 ♣ 6 5	
♠ J 9 7 5 2 ♡ 6 3 ◊ 10 8 4 ♣ 10 3 2		♠ K 4 ♡ Q 9 4 ◊ K Q 7 6 3 ♣ 9 8 7
	♠ A Q 10 8 ♡ K 7 ◊ 9 5 ♣ A K Q J 4	

doubleton, as looks likely from partner's lead, then you will have removed a vital dummy entry. The best declarer can do is take a spade finesse and ruff a spade in the dummy, but you can overruff and he will be one down.

38 If you defend passively you can see that declarer will make five spades, two hearts, two clubs and a diamond. Even if he started with ♣A-K-x, because you have only a doubleton and partner has no entry, declarer will have time to establish a heart for a club discard. Your only hope is that

Contract: 4♠ Lead: ♣Q	♠ A 6 5 ♡ Q J 10 8 ◊ A Q 4 ♣ 7 6 3	
♠ 7 4 ♡ 9 3 2 ◊ J 9 ♣ Q J 10 8 5 4		♠ K 8 ♡ A K 7 6 ◊ K 10 7 6 2 ♣ 9 2
	♠ Q J 10 9 3 2 ♡ 5 4 ◊ 8 5 3 ♣ A K	

declarer started with two hearts and three diamonds. You must switch to a diamond, playing partner for the ◊J, then play another diamond when you are in with the ♡K. Now you can cash the ◊K when you get in with the ♡A.

39 It looks as if declarer started with a doubleton club, and he must have a good heart suit, though there is room for your partner to have a defensive trick there. Your best chance of more tricks is in spades, but if you switch to a spade now and declarer has the ace he may be able to win,

Contract: 4♡ Lead: ♣5	♠ J 6 ♡ Q ◊ A K J 10 9 7 ♣ 9 4 3 2	
♠ K 10 7 ♡ 10 9 7 3 ◊ Q 4 ♣ Q 10 7 5		♠ Q 9 8 3 ♡ 5 2 ◊ 8 6 5 2 ♣ A K 6
	♠ A 5 4 2 ♡ A K J 8 6 4 ◊ 3 ♣ J 8	

draw trumps and run dummy's diamonds (if partner has the queen it will be dropping). A better plan is to neutralise dummy's diamonds by switching to that suit now. Declarer will be able to cash two diamonds for one spade discard, but when he plays a third diamond partner will ruff and play a trump. Now if partner has the ♠K, declarer must go down.

40 It is possible that partner has the ♡K and that a heart switch at this stage would enable him to win and play a club through but even if that is the case the correct defence will also work. You should switch to a *diamond*. You are hoping that declarer started with a doubleton, so by

Contract: 1NT Lead: ♠J	♠ K 5 ♡ 8 7 5 ◇ K Q 10 8 7 2 ♣ 8 3	
♠ J 10 9 6 ♡ A 6 4 ◇ 9 6 3 ♣ A Q 2		♠ A Q 3 ♡ Q 9 2 ◇ J 5 ♣ 9 7 6 5 4
	♠ 8 7 4 2 ♡ K J 10 3 ◇ A 4 ♣ K J 10	

switching to a diamond you force him to cash the suit immediately. And that will have a devastating effect on his hand. After cashing his diamonds he will have only three cards left, so must blank one of his kings, and you keep A-x in the suit he has blanked and singleton ace in the other suit. You must come to three tricks.

41 If you gaily continue spades, declarer will probably win and start on diamonds. You have to hope that partner has a diamond stopper, otherwise you have few prospects, but even so if declarer has the ♡A he will be home. You have to play partner for the ♡K or the ♣K. If partner had the ♣K he may have

Contract: 3NT Lead: ♠J	♠ 7 6 ♡ 5 ◇ A 10 8 7 6 4 3 ♣ A 9 7	
♠ J 10 5 4 ♡ K 7 4 ◇ Q J 5 ♣ 10 6 2		♠ A Q 9 3 ♡ Q J 6 2 ◇ — ♣ Q J 8 4 3
	♠ K 8 2 ♡ A 10 9 8 3 ◇ K 9 2 ♣ K 5	

preferred to lead your first suit, and declarer might not have tried 3NT, so it is better to play him for the ♡K. Switch to the ♡2. If declarer wins this he will have five losers when he loses to partner's ◇Q, so he must duck, and now the spotlight falls on your partner. He must switch back to spades.

42 Declarer's shape is surely 5-4-1-3 and you cannot take enough tricks in hearts to beat 3NT – at best you can take two hearts, a diamond and a club. When declarer next gets the lead he is going to play a club towards the dummy and you need to win that trick and take three more tricks

Contract: 3NT Lead: ♡3	♠ 7 2 ♡ 5 ◇ A K 10 9 5 3 ♣ K 9 5 3	
♠ J 5 ♡ 10 8 7 3 ◇ Q J 8 4 ♣ A 8 6		♠ K Q 10 9 ♡ K J 6 4 ◇ 6 2 ♣ 10 7 4
	♠ A 8 6 4 3 ♡ A Q 9 2 ◇ 7 ♣ Q J 2	

immediatcly. Your only chance is to switch to the ♠J. Partner has such good spot cards that he can overtake with the ♠Q. If declarer wins, when you take the ♣A there are three spades to take, to go with the diamond trick you already have. If declarer ducks the ♠Q, partner switches back to hearts and you take two hearts, one spade and one trick in each minor.

Chapter Eight

Counting the Hand

- **Counting Tricks**
- **Counting Points**
- **Counting Distribution**

One of the most important attributes of the good bridge player is his ability to count: count tricks, count points and count distribution. It should become second nature whether you are defending or playing the dummy, and it is often the key to the well-played hand or well-timed defence.

Counting Tricks

It is important, when you are declarer or a defender, to keep your target firmly in mind: how many tricks are you trying to take? how many tricks can you afford to lose?

Consider this example:

<table>
<tr><td></td><td>North
♠ K 6 5
♡ 9 6 5
◇ 9 8 7
♣ J 10 4 3</td><td></td></tr>
<tr><td>West
♠ J 8 3 2
♡ A J 2
◇ Q 10 4 3
♣ 9 6</td><td></td><td>East
♠ 10 7
♡ Q 10 8 7 4
◇ J 6 5 2
♣ A 5</td></tr>
<tr><td></td><td>South
♠ A Q 9 4
♡ K 3
◇ A K
♣ K Q 8 7 2</td><td></td></tr>
</table>

> **Try to work out where your defensive tricks are coming from.**

North/South's bidding was 2NT – 3NT. West led the three of diamonds. East played the jack and declarer won with the ace. Declarer now played a club to dummy's jack and East was in with the ace. What now?

In the event he woodenly returned a diamond and declarer soon made his contract – with an overtrick when West discarded spades.

East was wrong. He should have realised that it was unlikely that West had K-Q-x-x in diamonds: firstly, if that was the case declarer might well have ducked at trick one; and secondly, it is an unattractive lead into a Two No-trump opener. In addition, even if West did hold K-Q-x-x in diamonds, that made a total of only four defensive tricks because he knew West did not hold more than four diamonds. Consequently East should have switched to a heart as being the best chance of defeating the contract. This time he would have been rewarded by a two-trick defeat.

Counting Points

```
                    ♠  Q J 10 3        North
                    ♡  A K Q
                    ◇  Q 10 9
     West           ♣  J 9 4                      East

  ♠  8                                      ♠  K 7 6 4
  ♡  8 4 3 2                                ♡  J 10 7
  ◇  8 7 6 4 3 2                            ◇  5
  ♣  7 2                                    ♣  A K Q 8 3

                    ♠  A 9 5 2
                    ♡  9 6 5
                    ◇  A K J
        South       ♣  10 6 5
```

> Remember to work out how many points partner can have.

South opened a 12–14 No-trump and North jumped to Four Spades after Stayman had located the 4-4 fit. West led a club and East cashed three rounds of the suit. How should East be thinking?

Before you put that singleton diamond on the table, you should stop to count the points (though you should have done that as soon as you saw the dummy!). Dummy has 15, declarer 12 and you have 13. There is no room for partner to have a single high-card point. Your only chance of an extra trick is in trumps, so at trick four you should continue with a fourth round of clubs. When partner has the singleton eight your K-7-6-4 is promoted into a certain trick (try it and see!).

There are often more subtle clues from the bidding to help you count points. Here are some self-evident statements for you to bear in mind:

(1)   A hand that has failed to open the bidding when it had the opportunity to do so probably does not have 12 or more high-card points (HCP).

(2)   A hand that has passed his partner's one-level suit opening probably has fewer than 6 HCP.

(3)   A hand that has opened One of a suit probably does not have a balanced hand within its no-trump range.

Counting Distribution

	North	
	♠ A 10 3	
	♡ 10 4	
	◇ 10 6 5	
West	♣ A J 9 7 5	**East**
♠ —		♠ 8 6
♡ K Q 8 7 3		♡ A J 6 2
◇ Q 7 4 3 2		◇ K J 9
♣ 6 4 2		♣ K Q 10 8
	♠ K Q J 9 7 5 4 2	
	♡ 9 5	
	◇ A 8	
	South ♣ 3	

> Try to work out the distribution and then count the tricks for both sides.

When you know the distribution of a hand you can often work out how to defend. Sometimes you do not know the distribution precisely but can work out that a particular line of defence cannot cost.

South became declarer in Five Spades after West had had the opportunity to show a red two-suiter. West led the king of hearts and continued with a low heart to East's ace. How should East defend?

I guess East did what most of us would do: he switched to the king of clubs. Declarer won with the ace, ruffed a club, played the king of spades to the ace, ruffed a club, played a middle spade to the ten, ruffed a club, and now played a carefully preserved two of spades to dummy's three in order to reach the established fifth club.

East's defence was careless. Either South had a club loser or he didn't. There was no hurry to play the suit. If East switches to a trump when he is in, he removes an entry from dummy prematurely and the fifth club can never be established.

Try it Yourself

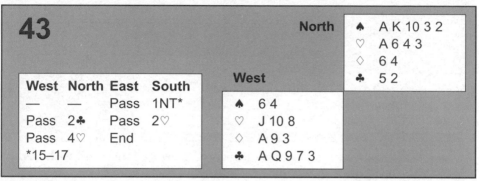

43

West	North	East	South
—	—	Pass	1NT*
Pass	2♣	Pass	2♡
Pass	4♡	End	
*15–17			

North
♠ A K 10 3 2
♡ A 6 4 3
♢ 6 4
♣ 5 2

West
♠ 6 4
♡ J 10 8
♢ A 9 3
♣ A Q 9 7 3

You lead the ♡J, which declarer wins in hand with the ♡K. He then cashes the ♡Q and plays the ♠A-K and ruffs a spade in hand. Over to you.

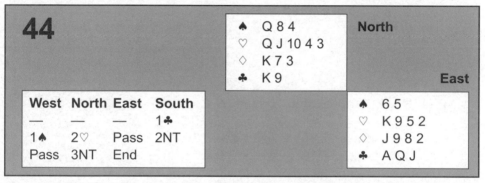

44

♠ Q 8 4
♡ Q J 10 4 3
♢ K 7 3
♣ K 9

North

East
♠ 6 5
♡ K 9 5 2
♢ J 9 8 2
♣ A Q J

West	North	East	South
—	—	—	1♣
1♠	2♡	Pass	2NT
Pass	3NT	End	

Against 3NT West leads the ♠J, which declarer wins in hand with the ♠K. He now plays the ♡A and a heart to dummy's queen. Plan the defence.

45

♠ A K 6 2
♡ A K Q 10
♢ 10 6
♣ J 10 7

North

East
♠ 5 4
♡ 8 6 2
♢ J 7 5 3
♣ A 8 5 3

West	North	East	South
—	1♡	Pass	1NT
Pass	2NT	Pass	3NT
End			

West leads the ♠J, won with dummy's king. Declarer plays the ♣J to partner's king and he plays another spade, won by declarer in hand with the ♠Q. Now a club to dummy's ten as West discards. How are you going to defend?

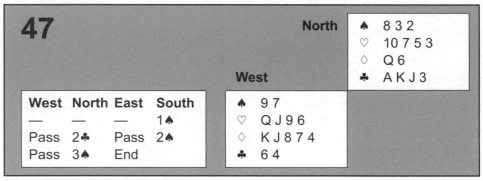

46

West	North	East	South
1◇	Pass	1♠	2♣
2♠	3♣	End	

North

♠ 9 8 2
♡ 10 6 3
◇ K J 9 4
♣ K 10 3

West

♠ A K Q 6
♡ 9 5 2
◇ A 7 6 3 2
♣ 7

You start off with three top spades, declarer following twice and ruffing the third. Declarer plays a club to dummy's king and a club to his ace, partner playing the ♣J while you discard a diamond. Now a low diamond. This time it is match-pointed pairs scoring. Do you duck or do you grab your ace?

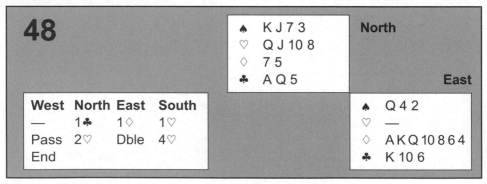

47

West	North	East	South
—	—	—	1♠
Pass	2♣	Pass	2♠
Pass	3♠	End	

North

♠ 8 3 2
♡ 10 7 5 3
◇ Q 6
♣ A K J 3

West

♠ 9 7
♡ Q J 9 6
◇ K J 8 7 4
♣ 6 4

You lead the ♡Q to partner's ace and partner returns the ♡4. Declarer wins the ♡K, cashes the ♠A, ♠K and ♠Q, partner following to all three, and plays a low heart. Over to you.

48

♠ K J 7 3
♡ Q J 10 8
◇ 7 5
♣ A Q 5

North

West	North	East	South
—	1♣	1◇	1♡
Pass	2♡	Dble	4♡
End			

East

♠ Q 4 2
♡ —
◇ A K Q 10 8 6 4
♣ K 10 6

Partner leads the ◇3. You win the ◇Q and continue with the ◇A, everyone following. What now?

Solutions

43 If you overruff you are wasting the power of your trumps. You know that if you discard, declarer will have to play a minor suit and you will be on lead. Then you can play a third round of hearts, thus drawing two of declarer's for one of yours. That way declarer will end up a trick

Contract: 4♡	♠ A K 10 3 2
Lead: ♡J	♡ A 6 4 3
	◇ 6 4
	♣ 5 2

♠ 6 4		♠ Q J 7 5
♡ J 10 8		♡ 5 2
◇ A 9 3		◇ 10 8 7 2
♣ A Q 9 7 3		♣ 10 8 4

	♠ 9 8
	♡ K Q 9 7
	◇ K Q J 5
	♣ K J 6

short. On the other hand, if you overruff you are endplayed. Your best defence would be to play a low diamond. Declarer can win and play another top diamond. You win and return a diamond, but declarer wins, pitching a club, and ruffs a diamond in dummy. Now he ruffs a second spade and can later reach dummy with a club ruff to cash his established spade for his tenth trick. So you must refuse to overruff.

44 It looks as if partner has the ♠A, so you can see that 3NT can be beaten if only partner can be persuaded to play a club when he is in with the ♠A. If you return a spade partner may well duck, and even if he wins he may play a diamond. You can see that declarer probably has only

Contract: 3NT	♠ Q 8 4
Lead: ♠J	♡ Q J 10 4 3
	◇ K 7 3
	♣ K 9

♠ A J 10 3 2		♠ 6 5
♡ 8 6		♡ K 9 5 2
◇ 6 5 4		◇ J 9 8 2
♣ 8 7 3		♣ A Q J

	♠ K 9 7
	♡ A 7
	◇ A Q 10
	♣ 10 6 5 4 2

eight tricks now: one spade, four hearts and three diamonds. So, switch to a high diamond now. Partner will realise that you have nothing in diamonds, so when he wins his ♠A, switching to a club will be his only chance of beating the game.

45 You can count nine tricks for declarer: three spades, three hearts and three clubs. If you are going to beat 3NT you need to take three tricks *now*. The only prospect is diamonds, and you need partner to hold the ◇A and ◇Q. If you switch to a low diamond, declarer will simply duck to ensure

Contract: 3NT	♠ A K 6 2
Lead: ♠J	♡ A K Q 10
	◇ 10 6
	♣ J 10 7

♠ J 10 9 8 3		♠ 5 4
♡ 9 5 3		♡ 8 6 2
◇ A Q 9 2		◇ J 7 5 3
♣ K		♣ A 8 5 3

	♠ Q 7
	♡ J 7 4
	◇ K 8 4
	♣ Q 9 6 4 2

his contract. No, to prevent him doing this you must switch to the ◇J.

46 As soon as you know that partner has only four spades, you know he can't have four hearts. Therefore declarer's distribution must be 2-4-1-6, and there is nothing to be gained by ducking the diamond. Go in with your ◇A, exit with a diamond, and let declarer play hearts himself.

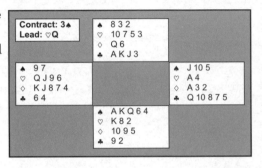

47 Count declarer's points. He has already turned up with 12, so surely has no more, and he certainly doesn't have an ace. Win your ♡J and switch to the ◇7. Partner will win with the ace and return the suit, and you can cash your ◇K and ◇J.

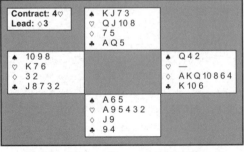

48 You are certainly endplayed and have to work out the least damaging switch. It does not look right to give a ruff and discard because declarer surely has a useful loser to discard from his hand. The danger with a spade is that you might not only give him a spade trick, but if the suit is 4-3-3-3 around the table he will be able to discard a club on the long spade. Your best chance is to switch to a club and hope that you can still take a heart and a spade trick to beat the game.

Chapter Nine

The Ruff and Discard

- **The Most Heinous Mistake You Can Make**
- **When to Give a Ruff and Discard**

One of the most heinous mistakes you can make at the
bridge table is to give a ruff and discard. Few errors will
receive less sympathy from partner. Yet sometimes giving a
ruff and discard is the only way to beat a contract. This
chapter gives some guidelines about this tricky situation.

The Most Heinous Mistake You Can Make

Generally speaking, it is not a good idea to give declarer a ruff and discard. Such a defence allows him to ruff in one hand while discarding a loser from the other. It is one of the great taboos of the game.

Count signals can help a lot in this situation, and even though we play attitude on partner's lead many inferences concerning count can be drawn.

```
                    Q 2
AK7643   [_____]   10 5
                    J 9 8
```

If you lead the ace-king of this suit against a suit contract and partner plays the ten and then the five, he is encouraging, and the only reason for such encouragement is that he has a doubleton and can possibly overruff the dummy.

If, on the other hand, he plays the five, then he is discouraging, and you would expect him to have a three-card holding. If you continue with a third round of the suit, declarer is likely to ruff in the dummy while partner follows and declarer discards a loser from his own hand.

Here is a full hand:

	North	
♠ Q 7 6		
♡ 8 7		
◇ K 6 5 4 2		
♣ J 10 6		

West		East
♠ J 8 5		♠ 9 4
♡ A K J 6 2		♡ 10 5 4 3
◇ Q 10		◇ J 9 3
♣ A 8 7		♣ 9 5 4 3

	South	
♠ A K 10 3 2		
♡ Q 9		
◇ A 8 7		
♣ K Q 2		

West leads the ace-king of hearts against South's Four Spades. If he switches to any suit at trick three declarer must go

Don't give a ruff and discard unless you are sure declarer has no useful discard.

down, losing a diamond and a club in addition to the two hearts. But if West continues with a third heart, then declarer ruffs in dummy, discarding a diamond from his hand. Now the diamond loser has escaped and he will make his contract.

It is important for East/West to understand their signalling correctly. If playing attitude signals, East should play a low heart at trick one. This is consistent with a holding of three or four cards and is merely sending a message that East does not have a doubleton. If East/West prefer to play count signals on partner's lead (which many do), then East plays his second highest heart and declarer has to guess whether this is from a doubleton or a four-card holding. On this occasion, declarer's play of the queen on the second round would lead West to guess that partner held four.

When to Give a Ruff and Discard

If all other avenues are hopeless, give a ruff and discard.

The main reasons for giving declarer a ruff and discard are:

(1)   because declarer clearly has no losers to discard; or
(2)   because declarer's trump holding is tenuous; or
(3)   because you are endplayed

Declarer has no losers to discard
One example of this type of hand is when all your honours are in front of dummy and you can see that all his finesses are working but he cannot. Here is an example:

	North	
	♠ A J 10 6	
	♡ A Q J 8 4 3	
	◇ A	
West	♣ J 3	East
♠ 7		♠ Q 8 5 4
♡ K 5 2		♡ 9 7
◇ J 9 4		◇ K 10 6 5
♣ A K 9 8 5 2		♣ Q 7 6
	South	
	♠ K 9 3 2	
	♡ 10 6	
	◇ Q 8 7 3 2	
	♣ 10 4	

North opened One Heart and raised South's One Spade response to Four Spades, ending the auction.

West leads the ace of clubs, and East discourages with the six. At trick two West continues with the king of clubs, and East follows with the seven. West can see that with the heart finesse working for declarer there is no future in either red suit. At trick three he continues with a third round of clubs.

Declarer should still succeed. He can discard a heart from the dummy while he ruffs in hand. Then he takes a heart finesse, now a spade to his nine and another heart finesse. But he might fall into the trap of ruffing in dummy and discarding a heart from his hand. Now, because of the 4-1 spade break he will have to go down. By giving the ruff and discard you have given him a losing option.

Declarer's combined trump holding is tenuous

When declarer's trumps are not quite what they should be, it is often a good idea to force him to ruff as often as possible, even if that means giving him a ruff and discard. We shall explore issues of trump control more fully in a later chapter.

When you are endplayed

Sometimes declarer plays a hand along 'elimination' lines, that is, he draws trumps, eliminates the side suits and throws a defender in to broach a suit for him. Occasionally, careful counting of the hand will reveal that declarer has a 4-4 fit in the suit you are about to broach. In such a circumstance, giving him a ruff and discard is the best option, since the card he will discard is not a loser.

Try it Yourself

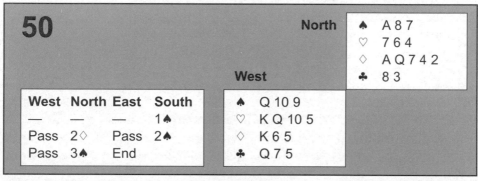

49

	♠ K J 7 6 2	North
	♡ Q 6	
	◇ 8 6	
	♣ A 10 6 2	East

	♠ 5
	♡ A J 5 4 3
	◇ Q 10 7 5 4
	♣ Q 7

West	North	East	South
—	—	Pass	1♠
Pass	4♠	End	

West leads the ♡2 and declarer plays low from dummy. You play the ♡J, which holds, and follow with the ace, declarer playing the ♡9 and ♡8, and partner the ♡7. You then switch to ◇5. Declarer plays the ◇A (partner playing the ◇9), draws two rounds of trumps, and exits with a diamond, partner playing the ◇3. How do you defend?

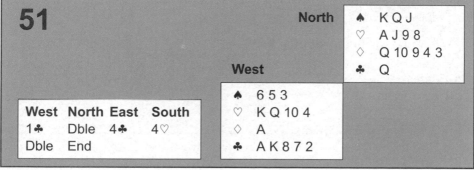

50

North	♠ A 8 7
	♡ 7 6 4
	◇ A Q 7 4 2
West	♣ 8 3

	♠ Q 10 9
	♡ K Q 10 5
	◇ K 6 5
	♣ Q 7 5

West	North	East	South
—	—	—	1♠
Pass	2◇	Pass	2♠
Pass	3♠	End	

You lead the ♡K, and continue the suit when East encourages. He wins the ♡A and plays a third heart. You are back in with your ♡Q. What now?

51

North	♠ K Q J
	♡ A J 9 8
	◇ Q 10 9 4 3
West	♣ Q

	♠ 6 5 3
	♡ K Q 10 4
	◇ A
	♣ A K 8 7 2

West	North	East	South
1♣	Dble	4♣	4♡
Dble	End		

You lead the ♣A, partner plays the ♣6 and declarer the ♣J. What now?

52

			North	♠	J 7 3
				♡	K J 10
				◇	Q J 10 7
				♣	10 7 5

West

West	North	East	South
—	—	—	1♠
Dble	1NT	2♡	2♠
3♡	3♠	Pass	4♠
End			

♠	—
♡	7 6 4 3
◇	K 5 4 2
♣	A K Q 8 3

You start off by leading three top clubs, declarer ruffing the third round. Declarer now plays a heart to dummy's king, partner playing the ♡9, and the ♠J, which holds. He follows with the ♠7 covered by the ♠8 and ♠9. Now a diamond towards dummy. Plan the defence.

53

			North	♠	3
				♡	J 4 2
				◇	A Q 5
				♣	K Q 9 8 7 2

West

West	North	East	South
—	—	—	1♡*
Pass	2♣	2♠	Pass
4♠	5♡	End	
*5-card major			

♠	J 9 5 2
♡	K 9
◇	J 10 8 4 2
♣	5 3

You lead the ♠2 to partner's ♠Q and declarer's ♠A. Declarer ruffs a spade in the dummy, plays three rounds of diamonds discarding a spade, and leads the ♡J, which runs round to your ♡K. Plan the defence.

54

♠	K 6 5	North
♡	8 4 3	
◇	K 4	
♣	K Q J 5 3	

West	North	East	South
—	—	—	Pass
Pass	1♣	2◇	2♡
Pass	Pass	3◇	Pass
Pass	3♡	End	

		East
♠	Q 2	
♡	7	
◇	A Q J 9 6 5 3	
♣	A 4 2	

West leads the ◇10 and you take the first two tricks in the suit, partner and declarer following to two rounds. What now?

Solutions

49 It looks very much as if partner started with ♡K-10-7-2 – his carding is consistent with such a holding and if declarer had started with three hearts then surely he would have ruffed one in the dummy. Partner's diamond play is also consistent with a four-card suit. Declarer's distribution is probably the same as dummy's, and the one thing you must not do is broach the club suit. Play either red suit and give declarer a ruff and discard, leaving him to guess clubs himself.

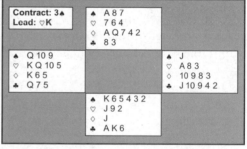

50 There are not many points left for partner to have. Declarer must have the ♣A-K to make up his opening bid, so there is no prospect of any tricks in the minors. The only chance is to find partner with the singleton ♠J, so play the thirteenth heart. Partner ruffs with the ♠J, forcing declarer to play the king and ensuring two more tricks for your ♠Q and ♠10.

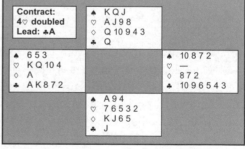

51 Perhaps your double was a little foolish, but you are unlucky to find such good trumps in the dummy. There is little room for partner to contribute anything in the way of high cards, partly because of the bidding and partly because his ♣6, clearly a middle card, suggests that he does not want a switch. The best chance is to continue clubs at every available opportunity. If you give declarer a ruff and discard now, another one when you get in with the ♢A, and a third one when you get in with one of your top hearts, declarer will have to go one down.

52 Declarer surely has three aces for his final raise to game over what was surely only a competitive 3♠ bid. He also must have exactly six spades; with fewer he would not have rebid 2♠, and with more he would have drawn East's last trump. Declarer is also known to have started with two

Contract: 4♠	♠ J 7 3
Lead: ♣A	♡ K J 10
	◊ Q J 10 7
	♣ 10 7 5

hearts, partner's ♡9 being the beginning of a peter. That leaves declarer with three diamonds and partner with a doubleton. The winning defence is to win the ◊K and lead a fourth round of clubs. If declarer ruffs in dummy he can no longer pick up your partner's ♠K, while if he ruffs in hand partner can discard his last diamond, so declarer cannot reach dummy without conceding a diamond ruff.

53 This is similar to the previous hand. In order for you to have any chance of defeating 5♡ partner must have the ♣A and ♡Q-x remaining. If you play a fourth round of diamonds, giving declarer a ruff and discard, you can stop him reaching dummy to pick up partner's hearts. If declarer discards

Contract: 5♡	♠ 3
Lead: ♠2	♡ J 4 2
	◊ A Q 5
	♣ K Q 9 8 7 2

from dummy, East will discard a low club. Now if declarer plays a club, East will win with the ace and give declarer another ruff and discard – in spades this time – and declarer has to concede another trump trick for one down.

54 There can be no rush to take any black-suit tricks. Perhaps playing a third round of diamonds will promote a second trump trick for partner if his holding is something like K-9-x-x. The other possibility, as in the actual layout, is that partner has a doubleton club. If you play your

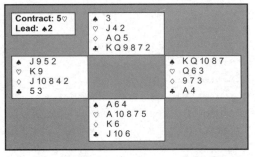

lowest diamond back he will know you have the ♣A and will discard from his doubleton. Then when he makes his trump trick he can lead a club and you will give him a ruff. Note that if partner actually holds the ♠A it can't disappear.

Chapter Ten

Trump Control

- ■ **The Power of the Ace of Trumps**
- ■ **Forcing Declarer to Lose Trump Control**

Generally speaking the declaring side have more trumps than the defenders, so the defenders must make their trumps work especially hard. When a defender is lucky enough to hold the ace of trumps he is particularly well placed to organise a defensive plan, especially if he has some length in trumps too and so can choose when he wins a trick with his ace.

When one defender has length in trumps, it may be possible to force declarer to ruff so that he has fewer trumps than that defender.

The Power of the Ace of Trumps

The ace of trumps is the most powerful card in the pack. When you hold it as a defender, it changes your perspective of the game. It makes leading a singleton more attractive because you know that even if you set up tricks for declarer you will regain the lead before he can cash them. It also means that you can plan the defence more easily, knowing that you cannot be denied the lead.

> When you hold the ace of trumps you don't need to give partner an immediate ruff.

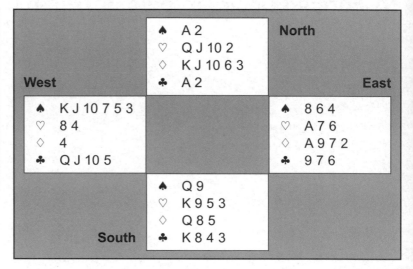

West opened Two Spades, showing 5–9 points with a six-card spade suit. North doubled for take-out, and South responded Three Hearts, by agreement showing some values, so North pressed on to Four Hearts.

West leads the four of diamonds, a probable singleton. If you, East, give partner a ruff immediately he will not be able to attack spades from his side. He will probably play a club. Declarer will win and play a trump. At some stage you will win your ace and switch to a spade, but it will be too late. Because you have the ace of trumps, there is no need to give partner his ruff immediately. Switch to a spade at trick two to establish partner's trick in that suit. Then, when you get in with the ace of hearts you can give partner a ruff and he can cash his spade trick.

<table>
<tr><td>When you hold the ace of trumps it often pays to withhold it for one round.</td></tr>
</table>

The following is a familiar layout of the trump suit:

```
              K Q x x
A x x      ┌──────────┐      x x
           └──────────┘
              J 10 x x
```

If declarer does not draw any trumps he may run into a defensive ruff. On the other hand, if he draws too many trumps he may not have enough left to ruff all his losers. What he would often like to do is draw just two rounds. Perhaps he plays the king of trumps from the dummy. If you helpfully win your ace, when he gets back in he can draw one more round and then go about his business, ruffing whatever losers he has left. If, on the other hand, you refuse to win your ace, he may have a problem. If he stops playing trumps he may lose a ruff, while if he plays another trump you will win your ace and draw a third round, perhaps leaving him a trick short.

Forcing Declarer to Lose Trump Control

When one of the defenders has four or more trumps and declarer is in a 5-3 or 6-2 fit, it is often profitable to force declarer to ruff in the long trump hand. If you can make him ruff often enough, you may be able to promote your small trumps into winners.

Here is a standard example:

	♠ K J 3 ♡ 9 6 ◇ J 7 6 2 ♣ A 10 5 3	**North**
West		**East**
♠ A 8 5 2 ♡ K Q J 7 3 ◇ 9 8 ♣ 8 4		♠ 6 ♡ A 10 5 4 2 ◇ Q 10 5 4 ♣ 9 7 6
	♠ Q 10 9 7 4 ♡ 8 ◇ A K 3 ♣ K Q J 2	
	South	

Against South's Four Spade contract you, West, start with two top hearts, declarer ruffing the second in hand. He now plays a low trump from hand. If you make the mistake of winning this trick, or the next, declarer will succeed, because when you play another heart, he can take the ruff in the dummy. What you must do is hold up the ace of trumps for two rounds. Then you can win the third round when dummy is out of trumps. Now play another heart and you have more trumps than declarer, so he must lose a second trump trick as well as two hearts.

> When the defenders hold some length in trumps, it is often sound to force declarer to ruff.

Did you spot declarer's mistake on this deal? He should have discarded a diamond at trick two instead of ruffing. Then he can ruff the next heart in the dummy, and the defence can no longer succeed.

Even if you had held a minor-suit singleton on this deal, it would have been right to lead a heart. When you have most of your side's defensive assets, along with four trumps, it usually works better to lead a long suit than a singleton. Your trump holding will probably be an embarrassment to declarer, and even if you can get a ruff or two, that might well make his life easier. On the other hand, with a very weak hand it is more appealing to lead a singleton because you know partner will have some entries.

Try it Yourself

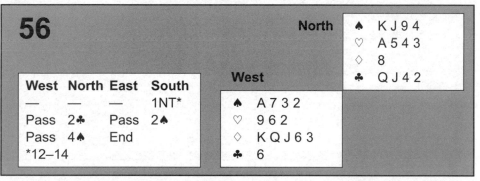

55

West	North	East	South
—	—	—	1♡
Pass	2NT	Pass	3♢
Pass	3♡	Pass	4♡
End			

North
♠ Q 9 8
♡ Q 5 4
♢ A Q 10
♣ Q 8 7 3

West
♠ 6 4 3
♡ A 9 3 2
♢ 8
♣ J 10 9 6 5

You lead the ♣J, which declarer ruffs. He now plays a heart. Plan the defence.

56

West	North	East	South
—	—	—	1NT*
Pass	2♣	Pass	2♠
Pass	4♠	End	
*12–14			

North
♠ K J 9 4
♡ A 5 4 3
♢ 8
♣ Q J 4 2

West
♠ A 7 3 2
♡ 9 6 2
♢ K Q J 6 3
♣ 6

You, West, lead the ♢K, and when it holds, continue the suit at trick two. Declarer ruffs in dummy and plays the ♠K. What now?

57

♠ 9 6 3 2
♡ K 7
♢ 4 2
♣ A Q J 10 4

North

East

West	North	East	South
—	—	1♠	3♡*
End			
*weak			

♠ A K 10 7 5
♡ A 6
♢ Q 7 5
♣ K 8 2

Partner leads the ♠4, and you win the ♠K as declarer plays the ♠J. Over to you.

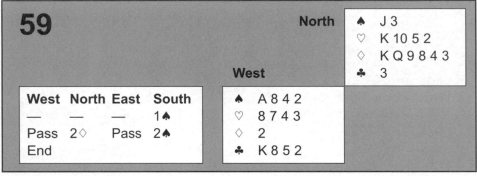

58

			North	♠ J 10 9 8
West	North	East	South	♡ J 10 7 4
—	—	—	1♠	◇ A 9 6 2
Pass	2♠	Pass	2NT	♣ 10
Pass	4♠	End		

West
♠ A 7 6 2
♡ Q 9 3 2
◇ Q 8
♣ J 7 5

Against 4♠ you lead the ♡2 to your partner's ace and he returns the ♡8, won by declarer's ♡K. Declarer leads a spade to dummy's jack, partner following, and a diamond to his ten and your queen. Plan the defence.

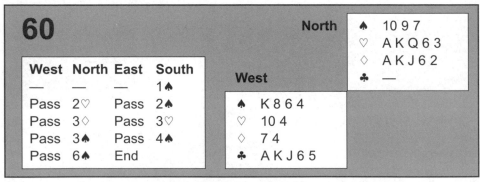

59

			North	♠ J 3
West	North	East	South	♡ K 10 5 2
—	—	—	1♠	◇ K Q 9 8 4 3
Pass	2◇	Pass	2♠	♣ 3
End				

West
♠ A 8 4 2
♡ 8 7 4 3
◇ 2
♣ K 8 5 2

You lead your singleton diamond, and partner wins the ace and returns the ◇5. Plan the defence.

60

			North	♠ 10 9 7
West	North	East	South	♡ A K Q 6 3
—	—	—	1♠	◇ A K J 6 2
Pass	2♡	Pass	2♠	♣ —
Pass	3◇	Pass	3♡	
Pass	3♠	Pass	4♠	
Pass	6♠	End		

West
♠ K 8 6 4
♡ 10 4
◇ 7 4
♣ A K J 6 5

Against South's slam you lead the ♣A, ruffed in dummy. Now declarer plays the ♠10 and runs it, partner discarding a small club. Plan the defence.

Solutions

55 It doesn't matter which trump you win on this deal, but when you win it you must continue clubs. Declarer has to ruff, and if he draws your trumps your partner will have two clubs to cash when he gets in with the ◇ K. If declarer takes a diamond finesse instead, your partner must

Contract: 4♡	♠ Q 9 8	
Lead: ♣J	♡ Q 5 4	
	◇ A Q 10	
	♣ Q 8 7 3	

♠ 6 4 3		♠ 10 7 5 2
♡ A 9 3 2		♡ 7
◇ 8		◇ K 6 5 2
♣ J 10 9 6 5		♣ A K 4 2

	♠ A K J	
	♡ K J 10 8 6	
	◇ J 9 7 4 3	
	♣ —	

continue clubs rather than give you a ruff. This is a good example of leading the long suit at trick one. On a diamond lead, 4♡ is cold.

56 On this deal it is important for you hold up your ♠A until the third round. Declarer has already been forced to ruff once in the dummy. If you win the first or second trump and play another diamond, he can take another ruff in dummy. But if you hold up until the third round, then

Contract: 4♠	♠ K J 9 4	
Lead: ◇K	♡ A 5 4 3	
	◇ 8	
	♣ Q J 4 2	

♠ A 7 3 2		♠ 8
♡ 9 6 2		♡ K 8 7
◇ K Q J 6 3		◇ A 7 5 2
♣ 6		♣ 9 8 7 5 3

	♠ Q 10 6 5	
	♡ Q J 10	
	◇ 10 9 4	
	♣ A K 10	

he will have to ruff your diamond continuation in hand and you will have one more trump than declarer. Better declarer play is to stop playing trumps when the 4-1 break is revealed, but now East/West will come to a club ruff, as well as a trick in each of the other suits.

57 The only switch to beat the contract is a low heart. Suppose instead East continues with a top spade; declarer ruffs and ducks a diamond. To stop the ruff, East must play the ♡A and another heart, and now declarer can draw trumps and concede a club. But what can declarer do

Contract: 3♡	♠ 9 6 3 2	
Lead: ♠4	♡ K 7	
	◇ 4 2	
	♣ A Q J 10 4	

♠ Q 8 4		♠ A K 10 7 5
♡ 8 4 2		♡ A 6
◇ K J 10 6 3		◇ Q 7 5
♣ 7 5		♣ K 8 2

	♠ J	
	♡ Q J 10 9 5 3	
	◇ A 9 8	
	♣ 9 6 3	

after the low trump switch? If he plays another, East will win and switch to a diamond, setting up two tricks to take when he is in with the ♣K. If instead he takes a club finesse, East ducks the first round. Now if declarer takes a second finesse, West can get a club ruff, while if instead declarer goes up with the ♣A, he cannot avoid two diamond losers.

58 Play another diamond. No doubt declarer will win and drive out your ♠A. But you must duck your ♠A again, and win the third round. Now there is one card in your hand that will beat the contract: the ♡Q. It forces declarer to ruff in hand, and he has no way to reach dummy to draw the last trump. No doubt he will try a diamond, but your ruff is the fourth defensive trick.

Contract: 4♠	♠ J 10 9 8	
Lead: ♡2	♡ J 10 7 4	
	◇ A 9 6 2	
	♣ 10	

♠ A 7 6 2		♠ 4
♡ Q 9 3 2		♡ A 8 6
◇ Q 8		◇ 7 5 4 3
♣ J 7 5		♣ Q 8 4 3 2

	♠ K Q 5 3	
	♡ K 5	
	◇ K J 10	
	♣ A K 9 6	

59 Partner's ◇5 is his lowest diamond, so it looks as if he has the ♣A. The trouble is that if you play a club to his ace and he gives you another ruff, you will be presented with a dilemma. If you play the ♠A and another spade, declarer can cash all dummy's diamonds, while if you play a low spade he can win, unblock the ♡A, ruff a club in dummy and cash the ♡K. Rather than play a club to partner's ace immediately you must first play a low spade. Suppose declarer cashes the ♡A and plays a spade. You win the ♠A and play the ♣2 to partner's ace. He continues with the ♣J. If declarer covers, you put partner back in with the ♣10 to get your diamond ruff; if declarer ducks then partner gives you a diamond ruff immediately. Declarer goes two down.

Contract: 2♠	♠ J 3	
Lead: ◇2	♡ K 10 5 2	
	◇ K Q 9 8 4 3	
	♣ 3	

♠ A 8 4 2		♠ 9
♡ 8 7 4 3		♡ Q J 9 6
◇ 2		◇ A 6 5
♣ K 8 5 2		♣ A J 10 9 6

	♠ K Q 10 7 6 5	
	♡ A	
	◇ J 10 7	
	♣ Q 7 4	

60 You must duck the spade. If you win and play a second club, declarer will ruff in the dummy and cross to hand with the ♡J to draw your trumps before cashing all his red-suit winners. But if you duck the spade he is in trouble. If he crosses to hand with the ♡J and ruffs his last club, he is stuck in the dummy and cannot get back to hand without allowing you to make a trick with your ♠8.

Contract: 6♠	♠ 10 9 7	
Lead: ♣A	♡ A K Q 6 3	
	◇ A K J 6 2	
	♣ —	

♠ K 8 6 4		♠ —
♡ 10 4		♡ 9 8 2
◇ 7 4		◇ Q 10 8 3
♣ A K J 6 5		♣ 10 8 7 4 3 2

	♠ A Q J 5 3 2	
	♡ J 7 5	
	◇ 9 5	
	♣ Q 9	

Chapter Eleven

Trump Promotion

- ## Simple Trump Promotion
- ## The Uppercut

In the previous chapter we were concerned with forcing declarer to ruff in order that our *long* trumps should make tricks. Here we will look at ways to promote the trick-taking capacity of our trump *honours*.

Simple Trump Promotion

A simple trump promotion can be demonstrated by the following layout:

```
              10 9 8 7
   Q 2      [===========]      6 3
              A K J 5 4
```

Left to his own devices declarer would probably drop your doubleton queen, but if partner can be left on play to lead a side suit in which both you and declarer are void, then a trick can be ensured for your queen. If declarer ruffs low you overruff, while if he ruffs high you will make your queen later.

A similar situation would arise if you had the singleton king and declarer had the ace-queen, or if you had J-x-x and declarer the ace, king and queen.

If declarer's honours are divided the situation is slightly different. Here is a full hand:

When dummy's trumps are weak, leading winners through declarer can promote trump tricks for partner.		

	North ♠ A 9 4 3 ♡ 7 6 2 ◇ A 9 5 4 2 ♣ Q	
West ♠ Q 10 ♡ K 5 ◇ Q J 6 3 ♣ A 8 6 5 4		**East** ♠ 8 7 ♡ A Q J 9 8 3 ◇ K 10 8 ♣ 9 2
	South ♠ K J 6 5 2 ♡ 10 4 ◇ 7 ♣ K J 10 7 3	

After a competitive auction, you, West, are on lead against Four Spades doubled, East having opened One Heart. You lead the king of hearts, which partner overtakes with the ace (your king might have been singleton) and continues with the queen and jack of hearts. Declarer realises that you had only a doubleton heart and has to decide what to do in the trump suit. As the cards lie he has no winning guess. If he ruffs low you will make your ten; if he ruffs with the jack you will make your queen now; and if he ruffs high you will make your queen later.

If declarer had had the ten of spades in hand as well as the jack he might have chosen to ruff high and then run the jack, playing you for the queen. So your defence might promote a trump trick even when your partner holds the queen!

A little bit of magic

> When your trump honour is supported by another high trump, refusing to overruff may gain you a trump trick.

Now look at a different layout:

```
                    7 6 2
      K 10 3     [          ]     8
                  A Q J 9 5 4
```

Again you lead your doubleton in a side suit and partner cashes a couple of rounds before playing a third round now that you and declarer are void. If declarer ruffs with the queen and you overruff, next time the ace and jack will drop your ten and no good will have been served. Or so you might think.

But look at the effect of your *refusing to overruff*. Now you have two trump tricks, the king and the ten.

There are several similar positions when you have a second high trump, perhaps A-9-x-x. And if partner has a singleton honour, then even quite lowly holdings can be promoted.

The Uppercut

The uppercut works when the player with the same shortage as declarer is the player to his right. Here is a standard position:

```
                    10 9 8 7
      Q 2        [          ]     J 3
                  A K 6 5 4
```

This time it is West who has the long suit, and declarer and East have doubletons. West cashes the ace and king and leads a third round (it doesn't matter whether North's card in the suit is a winner or a loser). East ruffs with the jack and declarer has no winning option. If he fails to overruff, the defence have made a trump trick to which they were not entitled; if he does overruff, West's queen is promoted.

Here is a full hand:

	North
♠ 9 8 5 4	
♡ 10 9 6 5	
◇ A K 7 2	
♣ 7	

West	East
♠ A 10 6	♠ 7
♡ K Q J 7 4	♡ A 3
◇ Q 6 3	◇ J 10 9 4
♣ 10 8	♣ 9 6 5 4 3 2

South	
♠ K Q J 3 2	
♡ 8 2	
◇ 8 5	
♣ A K Q J	

> **Ruffing with your highest trump may promote a trump trick for partner.**

Against South's Four Spades West leads the king of hearts. East overtakes with the ace and continues the suit. West can see that it is unlikely that the defenders have any minor-suit tricks. If East has a singleton trump honour then West has two trump tricks in any event, but if East has the singleton seven of trumps, then if he ruffs with it West's ten will be promoted into the setting trick. So West continues at trick three with a low heart. Note that even if East's trump is low so that West's trump is not promotable, nothing has been lost, and East's ruffing has prevented declarer from taking a discard.

Cash your outside winners first

The uppercut will gain you a trick only if declarer has no useful loser to discard. Suppose on the above hand that the contract had been *Three* Spades and declarer had had a loser in a side suit. Then, when East ruffed with the seven, declarer would have discarded his loser rather than overruff and the uppercut would not have gained anything.

Often there is nothing to be done about this, and at least the uppercut has not lost anything. But sometimes the defenders can prevent this by setting up outside tricks and cashing them before trying for the uppercut.

Try it Yourself

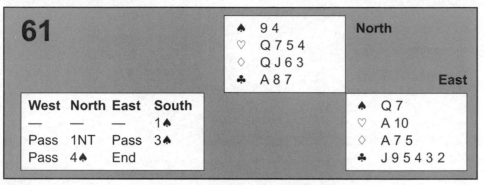

61

	♠	9 4	North
	♡	Q 7 5 4	
	◇	Q J 6 3	
	♣	A 8 7	East

West	North	East	South
—	—	—	1♠
Pass	1NT	Pass	3♠
Pass	4♠	End	

	♠	Q 7
	♡	A 10
	◇	A 7 5
	♣	J 9 5 4 3 2

Partner leads the ◇8 and declarer plays low from dummy. Plan the defence.

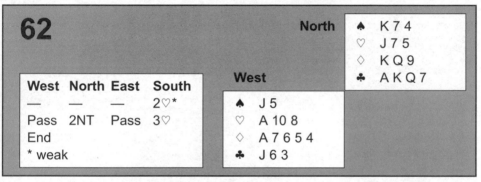

62

		North	♠	K 7 4
			♡	J 7 5
			◇	K Q 9
		West	♣	A K Q 7

West	North	East	South
—	—	—	2♡*
Pass	2NT	Pass	3♡
End			
* weak			

♠	J 5
♡	A 10 8
◇	A 7 6 5 4
♣	J 6 3

You lead the ♠J, which holds, and continue with another spade to dummy's king and partner's ace. Partner continues with the ♠Q, declarer ruffing with the ♡K. Over to you.

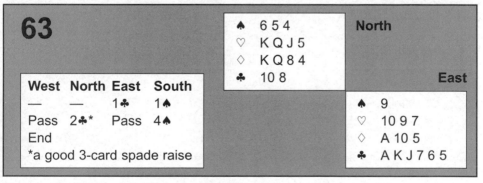

63

	♠	6 5 4	North
	♡	K Q J 5	
	◇	K Q 8 4	
	♣	10 8	East

West	North	East	South
—	—	1♣	1♠
Pass	2♣*	Pass	4♠
End			
*a good 3-card spade raise			

	♠	9
	♡	10 9 7
	◇	A 10 5
	♣	A K J 7 6 5

Partner leads the ♣9. Plan the defence.

64

	♠ K 9 4	North
	♡ 10 4	
	◇ K 6	
	♣ A J 9 8 3 2	East

West	North	East	South
—	—	—	1♠
2◇	3♣	Pass	3♡
Pass	4♠	End	

East:
♠ Q 7 5 2
♡ J 5
◇ 10 9 2
♣ K 7 6 4

West leads the ◇A followed by the ◇3, you contributing the ◇2 and ◇9 (suggesting a club value, remember) and declarer following twice. Declarer plays a low heart off the dummy to his queen, which partner wins with the ♡A and continues with the ♡2. Declarer wins the ♡K over your ♡J, and ruffs a heart in dummy with the ♠9. Over to you.

65

	♠ 3	North
	♡ 6	
	◇ K 7 6 2	
	♣ A K Q J 10 6 3	East

West	North	East	South
—	—	—	1◇
Pass	2♣	4♡	Dble
Pass	5◇	End	

East:
♠ A 2
♡ A K J 10 9 5 4
◇ Q J
♣ 5 4

West leads ♡3. Plan the defence.

66

				North	♠ A 5 4
					♡ A K 9 7 4
					◇ Q 9
					♣ J 10 4

West	North	East	South
—	—	—	1◇
Pass	1♡	2♠	3♣
3♠	Dble	Pass	4♣
Pass	4NT	Pass	5♡
Pass	6♣	End	

West:
♠ K 9
♡ 10 8 6 5 2
◇ 7 5 4 3
♣ K Q

You lead the ♠K which declarer wins with dummy's ace, partner playing the ♠Q. Declarer now plays the ♡A-K, discarding a spade while partner plays the ♡Q and ♡J. Declarer now plays the ♣J which runs round to your ♣Q, partner playing the ♣7. What now?

Solutions

51 Defensive prospects don't look too good on this hand. Dummy is maximum and your trump holding appears perfect for declarer. Clearly there are no defensive tricks to come from diamonds. Your best chance is to find partner with the ♡K; then you may be able to get a ruff or

Contract: 4♠	♠ 9 4
Lead: ◇8	♡ Q 7 5 4
	◇ Q J 6 3
	♣ A 8 7

♠ 10 5 3		♠ Q 7
♡ K 9 8 6 3		♡ A 10
◇ 9 8 2		◇ A 7 5
♣ Q 6		♣ J 9 5 4 3 2

	♠ A K J 8 6 2
	♡ J 2
	◇ K 10 4
	♣ K 10

promote a trump trick for partner if he has ♠10-x-x or ♠J-x. Win the ◇A, cash the ♡A and play a second heart to partner's king. A third round of hearts will enable you to ruff with the ♠Q, promoting partner's ten. There is no way of knowing how many hearts declarer started with. Maybe he will follow when you ruff, but it is better to be safe than sorry and ruff as high as you can.

52 If you overruff the spade, declarer will make his contract, losing just two spades, a heart and a diamond. But look what happens if you discard. Now your ♡A-10-8 must make two trump tricks whatever declarer does. This deal occurred at matchpointed pairs and North

Contract: 3♡	♠ K 7 4
Lead: ♠J	♡ J 7 5
	◇ K Q 9
	♣ A K Q 7

♠ J 5		♠ A Q 10 6 3 2
♡ A 10 8		♡ 6
◇ A 7 6 5 4		◇ 3 2
♣ J 6 3		♣ 8 5 4 2

	♠ 9 8
	♡ K Q 9 4 3 2
	◇ J 10 8
	♣ 10 9

took a conservative view in the bidding. You need to defend well to match those who beat 4♡.

63 Here declarer's game was always going one down, but at any form of scoring it is better to take the maximum number of tricks. Surely partner has a trump that can beat dummy's ♠6. So, win the ♣K, cash the ♣A and continue with the ♣5, your lowest club, asking partner to

Contract: 4♠	♠ 6 5 4
Lead: ♣9	♡ K Q J 5
	◇ K Q 8 4
	♣ 10 8

♠ Q 10 8		♠ 9
♡ 8 6 4 2		♡ 10 9 7
◇ 9 7 3 2		◇ A 10 5
♣ 9 3		♣ A K J 7 6 5

	♠ A K J 7 3 2
	♡ A 3
	◇ J 6
	♣ Q 4 2

return a diamond. When you win the ◇A you will continue with a fourth round of clubs, hoping to promote another trump trick for partner.

64 This hand is difficult. If you overruff the defence is over. When you overruff with the ♠Q, you tell declarer that partner has the ♠10. Say you return a club. Declarer will win, ruff a club to hand, ruff a heart with the ♠K and claim. But now suppose you refuse to overruff. Declarer will cash the

Contract: 4♠	♠ K 9 4
Lead: ◊A	♡ 10 4
	◊ K 6
	♣ A J 9 8 3 2

♠ 10		♠ Q 7 5 2
♡ A 9 8 2		♡ J 5
◊ A Q J 7 4 3		◊ 10 9 2
♣ Q 10		♣ K 7 6 4

	♠ A J 8 6 3
	♡ K Q 7 6 3
	◊ 8 5
	♣ 5

♣A, ruff a club and play another heart. If he ruffs high he has no more dummy entries and you must make your ♠Q and ♠7; if he ruffs low you overruff and play a trump and must later come to your ♠Q as well.

65 It looks as if partner started out with a singleton heart, in which case there are very good chances of scoring an uppercut. Provided that partner has a trump higher than dummy's seven, you can play a second heart and partner can force declarer to ruff with the ◊K, promoting your

Contract: 5◊	♠ 3
Lead: ♡3	♡ 6
	◊ K 7 6 2
	♣ A K Q J 10 6 3

♠ J 10 9 8 7 6 4		♠ A 2
♡ 3		♡ A K J 10 9 5 4
◊ 8 3		◊ Q J
♣ 9 8 7		♣ 5 4

	♠ K Q 5
	♡ Q 8 7 2
	◊ A 10 9 5 4
	♣ 2

◊Q-J into a trick. The trouble is, though, that if you do this straight away, when partner ruffs with his high trump declarer will surely discard dummy's ♠3 instead of overruffing and you will no longer be able to beat the game. Win the heart, *cash the ♠A*, and then play a low heart to make partner ruff.

66 Partner's ♣7 looks promising, since it suggests he may well have a higher spot card. You know that you don't have a spade trick to cash, and any diamonds can wait. If declarer's clubs were A-9-x-x-x you will probably make your ♣K on the next round anyway, but if declarer

Contract: 6♣	♠ A 5 4
Lead: ♠K	♡ A K 9 7 4
	◊ Q 9
	♣ J 10 4

♠ K 9		♠ Q J 10 8 7 6
♡ 10 8 6 5 2		♡ Q J
◊ 7 5 4 3		◊ 8 6
♣ K Q		♣ 9 8 7

	♠ 3 2
	♡ 3
	◊ A K J 10 2
	♣ A 6 5 3 2

is missing the ♣9 he will have no option but to drop your ♣K. However, if partner has the ♣9, you can succeed by playing a low heart now – if partner ruffs in with the ♣9, your ♣K will be promoted.

,

Chapter Twelve

Communications

- ## Maximising Your Own Side's Entries
- ## Attacking Declarer's Entries

Maintaining communications between the partnership hands is a very important aspect of card play, whether those hands are declarer and dummy or the two defending hands. This chapter is about preserving the communications between the two defending hands and trying to disrupt declarer's.

Maximising Your Own Side's Entries

As I mentioned in the *Introduction*, although this book is written in 17 chapters, defence is not so easily compartmentalised and there is considerable overlap. I first looked at the subject of Preserving Partner's Entries in *Chapter Six* in the section on Second Hand High. There we saw a situation where it was important to go in with an honour to stop partner's entry being knocked out.

Sometimes entries can be created by the unblocking of high cards.

	North	
	♠ A 9 2	
	♡ 9 7 6	
	◊ 9 5	
	♣ J 8 4 3 2	
West		**East**
♠ K J		♠ 10 8 7 6 5
♡ A Q 8 5		♡ J 10 4 2
◊ A Q 10 8 4		◊ J 3 2
♣ 10 6		♣ 9
	South	
	♠ Q 4 3	
	♡ K 3	
	◊ K 7 6	
	♣ A K Q 7 5	

> If you need partner to be on lead, consider discarding a high card in order to create an entry to his hand.

South opened One Club, West overcalled One Diamond, North raised to Two Clubs and South rebid Two No-trumps, ending the auction

West leads the five of hearts to the ten and declarer's king. Declarer now plays five rounds of clubs and West has to find three discards. Obviously he can't throw a spade. If he throws two hearts and a diamond he can never reach East's hand and is sure to be endplayed. If he throws three diamonds declarer exits with a heart, and after the hearts have been cashed East cannot play both a diamond and a spade through, so again West gets endplayed.

The winning answer is for West to throw a top heart and two diamonds. Now if declarer exits with a heart, West wins the first and puts East in with the jack. On the fourth round of hearts West can throw a spade, and now a high diamond through declarer beats the contract.

Another way to create entries into partner's hand is the Deschapelles Coup. This is the lead of an unsupported high honour in order to establish an entry to partner's hand. The most common position is:

```
                        A J
     Q 8 3     [==============]     K 10 5 2
                       9 7 6 4
```

East is on lead and is desperate to create an entry to his partner's hand, so he switches to the king. Whether declarer wins or ducks, West's queen has been established as an entry.

Attacking Declarer's Entries

> Be on the look-out for the opportunity to remove a dummy entry too early for declarer's liking.

The Deschapelles Coup has its parallel when it comes to attacking declarer's entries. In this situation it is known as the Merrimac Coup. A typical position would be:

```
                        A 4
     J 10 8 3   [==============]     K 5 2
                       Q 9 7 6
```

Here East is on lead and deems it vital to remove dummy's entry. He switches to the king and, again, whether declarer ducks or wins, the entry is removed.

There is not always the need for such drastic action, which is not without risk – perhaps declarer held Q-J-10-x-x in the suit, so switching to the king gives a trick and a tempo, and maybe dummy did not need the entry anyway. However, generally speaking, if dummy comes down with few high cards, it is a good idea to knock them out as soon as possible, because it is a lot easier to defend when you know that declarer can never reach dummy.

The corollary to this is that sometimes you would like to help declarer get to dummy, because all the finesses are wrong.

	North
♠ 7 4 2	
♡ 10 8 6 4	
◇ K Q J 5 3	
♣ 6	

West

| ♠ K 3 |
| ♡ K Q J |
| ◇ 10 8 7 |
| ♣ 10 9 8 4 3 |

East

| ♠ 9 8 |
| ♡ 9 3 |
| ◇ 9 6 4 2 |
| ♣ K Q J 5 2 |

South

| ♠ A Q J 10 6 5 |
| ♡ A 7 5 2 |
| ◇ A |
| ♣ A 7 |

> **Help declarer get to dummy when you know the finesses are wrong.**

North/South do well in the bidding, avoiding their poor heart fit and reaching Six Spades.

West leads the king of hearts which declarer wins with the ace. He then unblocks the ace of diamonds, cashes the ace of clubs and ruffs a club. He now plays three top diamonds discarding hearts, and West ruffs the last of these. If West now returns a heart declarer has no option but to drop the singleton king of spades. On the other hand, if West plays a club, giving a ruff and discard, declarer can reach dummy and may take the trump finesse.

Of course, declarer should not go wrong. He should ask himself why West is defending like this and drop the singleton king anyway, but it always pays to give the opposition as many chances as possible to go wrong.

Try it Yourself

67

	♠	7 5 3	North
	♡	9 7 5	
	◇	Q J 10 8 7	
	♣	A 4	East

				♠	A 6 4 2
West	North	East	South	♡	10 6 4 2
—	—	—	2NT	◇	K 6 4
Pass	3NT	End		♣	K 6

Your partner leads the ♠J which you win with the ♠A, declarer playing the ♠Q. Plan the defence.

68

	♠	K 10 2	North
	♡	K 4	
	◇	J 6 3	
	♣	A Q 10 6 5	East

				♠	A Q 5 4
West	North	East	South	♡	A
—	—	1◇	1♡	◇	A Q 10 9 4
Pass	2♣	Pass	2♡	♣	9 8 3
Pass	3♡	End			

West leads the ◇8 against South's 3♡. Declarer plays low from dummy and you play the ◇9, which declarer wins with the king. He now plays a heart to dummy's king and your ace. Plan the defence.

69

	♠	J 4 2	North
	♡	9 6	
	◇	7 2	
	♣	A Q 10 9 8 3	East

				♠	9 8 6 5
West	North	East	South	♡	Q 2
—	—	—	1♡	◇	Q 10 5 3
Dble	2♣	Pass	2♡	♣	7 6 4
Pass	Pass	2♠	Pass		
Pass	3♡	End			

Against 3♡, West leads the ♠A, declarer dropping the ♠Q, and switches to the ♣2. Declarer rises with the ♣A, dropping his ♣K, cashes the ♣Q discarding the ♠10, and leads the ◇2 from the dummy. Over to you.

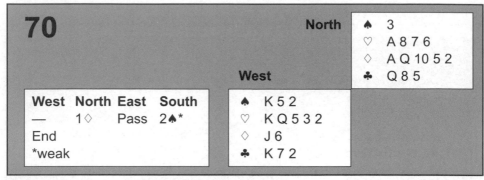

70

West	North	East	South
—	1◊	Pass	2♠*
End			
*weak			

North
- ♠ 3
- ♡ A 8 7 6
- ◊ A Q 10 5 2
- ♣ Q 8 5

West
- ♠ K 5 2
- ♡ K Q 5 3 2
- ◊ J 6
- ♣ K 7 2

You lead the ♡K, which declarer wins in dummy with the ♡A, East playing the ♡J. He now plays a spade to his queen and your king. Over to you.

71

West	North	East	South
—	2♣	Pass	2◊
Pass	3◊	Pass	3NT
Pass	4♣	Pass	4♠
Pass	6◊	End	

North
- ♠ Q
- ♡ A K
- ◊ A K Q J 10 2
- ♣ A K J 10

West
- ♠ A J 10 6 4
- ♡ 10 9
- ◊ 9 7 4
- ♣ 9 7 2

It is matchpointed pairs scoring, so you decide to lead the ♠A. Partner plays the ♠8. How do you continue?

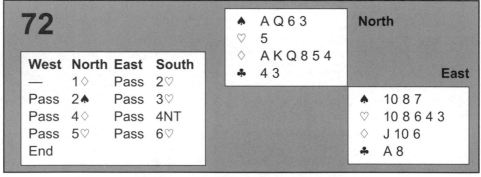

72

West	North	East	South
—	1◊	Pass	2♡
Pass	2♠	Pass	3♡
Pass	4◊	Pass	4NT
Pass	5♡	Pass	6♡
End			

North
- ♠ A Q 6 3
- ♡ 5
- ◊ A K Q 8 5 4
- ♣ 4 3

East
- ♠ 10 8 7
- ♡ 10 8 6 4 3
- ◊ J 10 6
- ♣ A 8

West leads the ♣Q and you win your ace. Plan the defence.

Solutions

67 You must switch to the ♣K, a Merrimac Coup. Priority must be given to destroying the entry to dummy's diamonds. Unless declarer began with four diamonds, switching to the ♣K stops the run of the suit. The best declarer can do is take a diamond finesse to make two tricks

Contract: 3NT Lead: ♠J	♠ 7 5 3 ♡ 9 7 5 ◇ Q J 10 8 7 ♣ A 4	
♠ J 10 9 8 ♡ J 8 ◇ 9 3 2 ♣ J 10 7 5		♠ A 6 4 2 ♡ 10 6 4 2 ◇ K 6 4 ♣ K 6
	♠ K Q ♡ A K Q 3 ◇ A 5 ♣ Q 9 8 3 2	

in the suit, while if the ♣A remains in the dummy he can make four diamond tricks simply by playing the ◇A and another.

68 There are two possible lines of defence: (1) cash two diamonds and play a third round, hoping to promote a trump in partner's hand, or (2) play one top diamond and then give partner a diamond ruff so he can play a spade through the dummy and you can take two spade tricks. The

Contract: 3♡ Lead: ◇8	♠ K 10 2 ♡ K 4 ◇ J 6 3 ♣ A Q 10 6 5	
♠ J 8 7 3 ♡ 7 6 3 2 ◇ 8 2 ♣ J 7 2		♠ A Q 5 4 ♡ A ◇ A Q 10 9 4 ♣ 9 8 3
	♠ 9 6 ♡ Q J 10 9 8 5 ◇ K 7 5 ♣ K 4	

bidding makes this second plan a better prospect. Remember to play the ◇10 for partner to ruff, so that he knows to play a spade and not a club.

69 If you play a low diamond, you have let declarer make 3♡. Your partner will win and cannot attack hearts profitably from his side. He either has to give up a trump trick or allow declarer to ruff a diamond in the dummy. You need to be there with the ◇Q or ◇10. If declarer ducks you

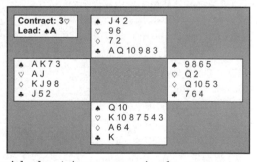

Contract: 3♡ Lead: ♠A	♠ J 4 2 ♡ 9 6 ◇ 7 2 ♣ A Q 10 9 8 3	
♠ A K 7 3 ♡ A J ◇ K J 9 8 ♣ J 5 2		♠ 9 8 6 5 ♡ Q 2 ◇ Q 10 5 3 ♣ 7 6 4
	♠ Q 10 ♡ K 10 8 7 5 4 3 ◇ A 6 4 ♣ K	

switch to a trump, while if he wins with the ◇A you can win the next round with your remaining honour.

70

Assuming declarer has ♠A-Q-J-x-x-x and little else, you can see one spade, one heart, one diamond and two clubs as potential defensive tricks and the most likely place to find another is if you can get a diamond ruff. Partner's ♡J might be a singleton, but provided declarer

Contract: 2♠ Lead: ♡K	♠ 3 ♡ A 8 7 6 ◇ A Q 10 5 2 ♣ Q 8 5	
♠ K 5 2 ♡ K Q 5 3 2 ◇ J 6 ♣ K 7 2		♠ 9 7 4 ♡ J 10 ◇ K 8 7 ♣ A J 9 6 4
	♠ A Q J 10 8 6 ♡ 9 4 ◇ 9 4 3 ♣ 10 3	

does not have a singleton diamond, he can't get back to hand quickly to draw trumps, so you can give partner a ruff later. You need to switch to a diamond now. But if you play the ◇J, declarer will play the ◇Q and partner will win his ◇K. Now the ◇9 is a vital entry to declarer's hand so he can draw trumps before you get your ruff. Switch instead to the ◇6, and now declarer cannot succeed.

71

Continue with the ♠J. Because you have nothing you are quite happy for declarer to get to hand to take the club finesse – you know it will lose. But if he has to play from his hand, partner's queen might drop.

Contract: 6♡ Lead: ♠J	♠ Q ♡ A K ◇ A K Q J 10 2 ♣ A K J 10	
♠ A J 10 6 4 ♡ 10 9 ◇ 9 7 4 ♣ 9 7 2		♠ 9 8 5 2 ♡ Q 8 6 4 3 2 ◇ 6 ♣ Q 5
	♠ K 7 3 ♡ J 7 5 ◇ 8 5 3 ♣ 8 6 4 3	

72

You have just won an ace and, unless declarer is psychic, you have a trump trick to come. You must concentrate on protecting that trump trick. Once declarer discovers the bad trump break he may be able to shorten his trumps by ruffing in hand and then play winners from dummy. At

Contract: 6♡ Lead: ♣Q	♠ A Q 6 3 ♡ 5 ◇ A K Q 8 5 4 ♣ 4 3	
♠ J 9 4 2 ♡ — ◇ 9 3 2 ♣ Q J 10 7 5 2		♠ 10 8 7 ♡ 10 8 6 4 3 ◇ J 10 6 ♣ A 8
	♠ K 5 ♡ A K Q J 9 7 2 ◇ 7 ♣ K 9 6	

some stage you will have to ruff and he can overruff and then draw your trumps (a 'trump coup'). You must return a diamond or a spade now to take an entry out of dummy, and now this play can no longer succeed.

Chapter Thirteen

Ducking

- **Count Signals Help You Duck**
- **Declarer Leads a Singleton from Dummy**
- **Ducking to Preserve Communications**
- **Ducking to Give Declarer a Guess**

Ducking is an essential tool in cardplay – both for declarer and for defenders. There are several reasons for ducking as a defender. First, it helps maintain communications; second, it makes declarer's life more difficult; and, third, concealing the whereabouts of an honour can give declarer a losing option in a suit.

Count Signals Help You Duck

In *Chapter One* we looked at count signals. One of the reasons for giving count when declarer plays a suit is so that you know when to duck and when to win a trick. If declarer has K-Q-J-x in one hand facing x-x-x in the other, whether this is in no-trumps or a suit contract, whatever the entry position, it is a matter of good technique to duck until the third round.

> **Give count so partner knows when to duck.**

If declarer leads towards K-Q-x-x, it is a matter of good technique to duck your ace. If you are in front of dummy and declarer has a singleton it is still often right to duck because by going in with the ace you give declarer two tricks when before he had only one. If he has more than a singleton, then it is right to duck because he will now need to use up an entry to get back to hand to lead a second card in the suit. If you are over the dummy, provided you know declarer did not start with a singleton (and partner's count signal should help you here), it is still right to duck because declarer will probably use up an entry getting back to hand to play the suit again, hoping that your partner held the ace.

It is still correct to play like this if the K-Q-x-x is in the concealed hand, but it is harder because you have to guess declarer's holding. You may feel that you would look silly to duck and find that declarer just had the unsupported king. But generally speaking, if declarer plays this suit early on, he is likely to have the king and queen.

Declarer Leads a Singleton from Dummy

When declarer in a suit contract leads a singleton from the dummy it is very tempting to go in with the ace, and indeed this can be the right play. But often it works better to duck, particularly when you have length in the suit and there are not too many trumps in the dummy.

Consider these layouts:

(1)	x		(2)	x	
K 10 x		A x x x	K 10 x x		A x x
	Q J 9 x x			Q J 9 x x	

If you rise with the ace on (1) when the singleton is played from dummy, declarer can take a ruffing finesse on the next round and then the suit will be good. If you play low, declarer will need to ruff three times in the dummy to establish the suit. With (2) the situation is not quite so critical because declarer will need two ruffs in dummy to establish the suit whether you go in with your ace or play low.

Obviously you do not know declarer's holding. It is possible that he will play his unsupported king and that that was the only way to make his contract. But this is rare. Much more often you will make his life more difficult by withholding your ace.

Ducking to Preserve Communications

> If defensive entries are in short supply, ducking can help to preserve them.

This is another example of where obtaining a count of the hand can tell you what to do. We covered one basic position in *Chapter Five* where we led fourth highest from A-x-x-x-x against a no-trump contract. Partner won the king and returned his original second or fourth highest. Where we know he started with K-x-x, we can duck in order to keep communication lines open. If we win the ace and clear the suit we need a sure quick entry.

Another situation where it is right to duck in order to preserve communications is when partner has led a doubleton against a suit contract and you hold the ace. If you are the one with the entries, there is no problem – simply win and continue the suit, but if you have no outside entry, the only way partner can reach your hand for you to give him a ruff is in the suit originally led.

Again, this is not a clearcut situation because it is possible that your partner has led a singleton, in which case winning immediately and returning the suit is what is called for. Obviously you must use the bidding to guide you, but in my experience, the doubleton is much more frequent.

Ducking to Give Declarer a Guess

Try to make life difficult for declarer.

There are some situations where, if you win a trick, declarer has no option but to play in a certain way on the second round, while if you duck he has a losing option.

Look at this position:

<pre>
                    7 6 4
     A 9 5   ▭▭▭▭▭   J 8 3
                    K Q 10 2
</pre>

Declarer leads small from dummy and plays the king from his hand. If you win the ace, when he plays the suit again he has no real choice but to play the ten, finessing against your partner's jack. But, if you play low when he plays the king, next time he leads the suit he has a guess. Should he play East for the ace or the jack? And when he has a guess he will go wrong some of the time.

Ducking to Avoid Committing Yourself

Suppose your partner leads a highish card against a no-trump contract, probably a MUD lead. Maybe there is K-Q-J in the dummy and you have A-x-x. Sometimes it is clear how to proceed, in which case it is fine to win your ace and go about your business, but more often there is no obvious line of defence. In such circumstances it is better to duck this trick until you know more about the hand.

Try not to commit yourself to a particular line of defence until you know what to do.

Try it Yourself

73

	♠ 3	North
	♡ K Q 5 4	
	♢ K 6 5 2	
	♣ 7 6 3 2	East

West	North	East	South
—	—	—	1♡
Pass	3♡	Pass	4♡
End			

East:
♠ A 7 6 2
♡ 7 2
♢ 8 4 3
♣ A J 10 9

Partner leads the ♢Q which declarer wins in dummy with the king. He now plays the ♠3. Are you ready for this? Do you duck or do you win?

74

North:
♠ K Q J 10 7 3
♡ Q 9
♢ A 5
♣ A 5 3

West:
♠ A 9 8 6
♡ K 8 3
♢ 9 8 4 3
♣ Q 2

West	North	East	South
—	1♠	Pass	1NT
Pass	2NT	Pass	3NT
End			

You lead the ♢8 on which dummy plays low and partner wins with the ♢K. He switches to the ♣9, covered by the jack, queen and ace. Declarer now plays the ♠K from the dummy, discarding a heart from hand. Over to you.

75

North:
♠ K 6 4
♡ 8 5
♢ A 6 3 2
♣ A K 8 5

East:
♠ A 7 2
♡ A 9 6 3 2
♢ 8 4
♣ 10 4 2

West	North	East	South
—	—	—	1NT*
Pass	3NT	End	
*10–12			

Your partner leads the ♡J and, as this is consistent with K-J-10-x, you play the ace. Declarer plays low and wins your heart continuation with the king. He now plays a spade to dummy's king. How do you defend?

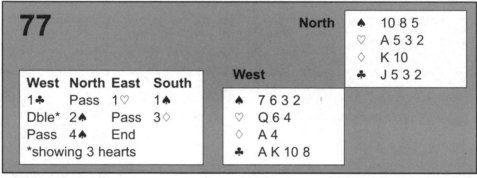

76

West	North	East	South
—	—	—	1♠
Pass	2♣	Pass	2NT*
Pass	3♠	Pass	4♠
End			
*15–19			

North
- ♠ 10 9 8
- ♡ A 9 5
- ◇ 10 7 3
- ♣ A K 8 5

West
- ♠ A 4
- ♡ J 10 8 6
- ◇ A J 6 2
- ♣ 10 6 3

You lead the ♡J which declarer wins in hand with the queen, your partner playing the ♡2. Declarer now plays a club to dummy's king, East playing the ♣9, and a spade to his king. Over to you.

77

West	North	East	South
1♣	Pass	1♡	1♠
Dble*	2♠	Pass	3◇
Pass	4♠	End	
*showing 3 hearts			

North
- ♠ 10 8 5
- ♡ A 5 3 2
- ◇ K 10
- ♣ J 5 3 2

West
- ♠ 7 6 3 2
- ♡ Q 6 4
- ◇ A 4
- ♣ A K 10 8

You lead the ♣A and at trick two, after partner's signal with the ♣7, you continue with the ♣K which declarer ruffs. Declarer plays a diamond. Do you duck or do you win?

78

West	North	East	South
—	—	—	1♡
Pass	3♡*	Dble	4♡
End			
*pre-emptive			

North
- ♠ 9 5 3
- ♡ J 8 7 3
- ◇ J 9 5 4
- ♣ J 2

West
- ♠ 8 7 6
- ♡ 5 2
- ◇ K Q 8 7 3
- ♣ Q 7 6

At trick one you lead the ◇K – not a success when partner plays the ◇6 and declarer wins with the ace. Declarer now draws trumps in two rounds and plays the ◇2. How do you defend?

Solutions

73 You must duck the ♠A. Although you will be wrong some of the time – generally when all declarer was concerned about was top losers, so puts in the ♠K. Much more often, playing low will succeed. If declarer has a king-jack guess he will probably guess wrong; even if he has K-x-x-x he

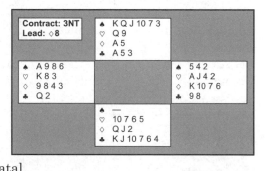

may duck, playing your partner for A-x-x; if he has queen-jack when you duck he needs to ruff all the suit in the dummy while if you play the ♠A he can take a ruffing finesse through your partner. The only way for you to beat 4♡ is for you to duck and declarer to guess wrong. Now a trump switch will beat the game.

74 This time you must win. There is no real point in holding up. You know declarer has plenty of tricks: five spades, two diamonds and at least two clubs. Your only chance is to take three heart tricks. So win the ♠A and switch to a heart now (the ♡K makes it easy for partner). This time ducking one spade would be fatal.

75 You must not play your ♠A. If you do you will have no entry for your long hearts. Duck your ♠A smoothly and declarer will surely play a spade back to his ten and partner's jack. Partner can now clear the hearts while you still have the ♠A as an entry. This play comes up quite often. Provided you duck smoothly, declarer will nearly always go wrong on the next round, which gives defenders the choice of which of them wins the first round of the suit.

76

You must duck the spade. Declarer has gone to some trouble to cross to dummy to play the suit so it is probable that your partner has the ♠J. If you win your ♠A now, declarer has little choice but to cross back to dummy to run the ♠10. But if you duck your ♠A, he has to guess on the second round of the suit.

Contract: 4♠	♠ 10 9 8
Lead: ♡J	♡ A 9 5
	◊ 10 7 3
	♣ A K 8 5

♠ A 4		♠ J 7 2
♡ J 10 8 6		♡ 7 3 2
◊ A J 6 2		◊ 9 8 4
♣ 10 6 3		♣ Q J 9 2

	♠ K Q 6 5 3
	♡ K Q 4
	◊ K Q 5
	♣ 7 4

77

If you play a small diamond, declarer will win in dummy and run the ◊10 to you. Best is for you to continue clubs, but this will not succeed for declarer will discard a heart from hand. If you now persist with clubs, he can play on a complete cross-ruff, making a trick each in

Contract: 4♠	♠ 10 8 5
Lead: ♣A	♡ A 5 3 2
	◊ K 10
	♣ J 5 3 2

♠ 7 6 3 2		♠ 4
♡ Q 6 4		♡ K J 10 9
◊ A 4		◊ J 8 7 5
♣ A K 10 8		♣ Q 7 6 4

	♠ A K Q J 9
	♡ 8 7
	◊ Q 9 6 3 2
	♣ 9

hearts and diamonds and eight trump tricks. But if you go in with the ◊A immediately and play a third club, he is stumped. If he discards a heart, you switch to a trump and the diamond suit is blocked. He cannot come to a tenth trick.

78

Don't let dummy's extreme weakness put you off. You still need to be careful to beat this game. You must duck the diamond and hope that partner started with ◊10-6. If you rise with the ◊Q you give declarer two more diamond tricks in the dummy, while if you duck you give him only one and he

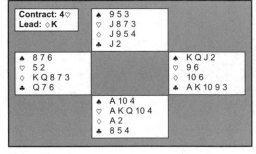

Contract: 4♡	♠ 9 5 3
Lead: ◊K	♡ J 8 7 3
	◊ J 9 5 4
	♣ J 2

♠ 8 7 6		♠ K Q J 2
♡ 5 2		♡ 9 6
◊ K Q 8 7 3		◊ 10 6
♣ Q 7 6		♣ A K 10 9 3

	♠ A 10 4
	♡ A K Q 10 4
	◊ A 2
	♣ 8 5 4

still has to lose four tricks in the black suits.

Chapter Fourteen

Blocking and Unblocking

- **Unblocking Partner's Suit**
- **Unblocking to Preserve Partner's Entries**
- **Unblocking to Avoid the Endplay**

As we have seen before, bridge is a partnership game, and the key to good defence, as well as good declarer play, is for the two partners to be able to move freely from one hand to the other. Blocking plays seek to hamper the other side's movements, while unblocking plays are an attempt to improve one's own.

Unblocking Partner's Suit

> Make sure that the card you return will not lead to a blockage in partner's suit.

In *Chapter Five* we looked at returning partner's suit and learned to return the original second or fourth highest in order to get a count of the hand . However, this is not something that can be applied blindly. Suppose this is the layout in a no-trump contract:

```
                    7 5
    A 8 6 4 3    [          ]    K 10 9 2
                    Q J
```

Partner leads the four and East plays the king, which holds. If he continues with the two the suit will be blocked and it will no longer be possible to take the first five tricks.

In this type of situation you must give priority to unblocking: return the ten and hope partner works it out.

Unblocking to Preserve Partner's Entries

We saw some problems of this sort in *Chapter Eleven*, but there are some fairly common situations. One thing to remember is that declarer is not psychic. If he bashes out the ace of his trump suit it is very unlikely that he had a finesse position – and if he did he would not need that finesse to make his contract.

```
                    ♠ K 9 2        North
                    ♡ J 6 5 4
                    ◊ A
    West            ♣ A K Q 4 3              East
    ♠ A J 10 7 4                        ♠ 6 3
    ♡ K 3                               ♡ Q 10 9
    ◊ Q J 10 5 2                        ◊ K 9 8 4
    ♣ 6                                 ♣ J 10 9 7
                    ♠ Q 8 5
                    ♡ A 8 7 2
                    ◊ 7 6 3
          South     ♣ 8 5 2
```

> If declarer cashes an ace, it is unlikely that unblocking your king will cost the contract.

North opened the bidding with One Club and South responded One Heart. West bid Two Hearts to show a good hand with five cards in both spades and diamonds, and North closed the auction with a leap to Four Hearts.

West led his singleton club and South paused to consider. If West's distribution was 5-2-5-1, as expected, he could not afford to duck a trump, because then West would get a ruff with his small trump and there would still be two trump losers and the ace of spades.

So declarer played ace and another heart. If West plays 'normally' he is on lead at the second trick, and plays a diamond. Declarer wins in dummy, plays off his top clubs and ruffs the fourth round in hand. Now he ruffs a diamond and plays the fifth round of clubs, discarding a spade. Now a spade from the dummy establishes a trick in the suit and he makes ten tricks when he ruffs his last diamond.

Now suppose West unblocks his king of hearts under the ace. If declarer reverts to clubs straight away he is down. So he must play a second trump and now East draws another round. East then switches to a diamond. Declarer wins in dummy and plays off his clubs as before, ruffing the fourth round. Then he plays a spade to the dummy and cashes his long club, but he has only been able to ruff one diamond in the dummy and ends up a trick short.

Unblocking to Avoid the Endplay

When you are the possessor of most of the defensive assets you have to be particularly careful not to allow yourself to be endplayed. Often the play develops in such a way that declarer's plan is obvious. If you can see that he cannot go wrong if he puts you on lead, then you must do whatever is necessary to make sure you are not left on lead.
Consider the following example:

	North
♠ A 8 7 6 5	
♡ Q 10	
◇ K 7 3	
♣ 8 7 4	

West

♠ Q 9	♠ 3
♡ K J 8 7 3	♡ 9 5 4 2
◇ J 10 9	◇ 8 6 5 4
♣ Q J 3	♣ 10 9 6 2

East

	South
♠ K J 10 4 2	
♡ A 6	
◇ A Q 2	
♣ A K 5	

> If you have most of your side's high cards you may get endplayed unless you can create an entry to partner's hand.

Here South was declarer in Six Spades. He had opened Two No-trumps, and jumped to Four Spades when his partner transferred with Three Hearts. Thereupon North had simply used Blackwood to make sure that there were not two aces missing.

West led the jack of diamonds. Declarer won in hand, drew two rounds of trumps, and played the ace and king of clubs. West was alert to the danger and on the ace of clubs played the queen. East co-operated by playing the ten, so West was happy to unblock the jack under the king. Declarer next cashed his diamonds and then exited with a club. Because of West's careful unblocking East won this trick and a heart switch doomed the slam.

Try it Yourself

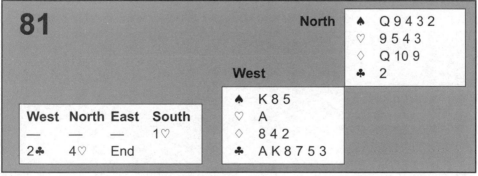

79

			North	♠	9 3
				♡	9 7 6 3 2
				◇	K 5 4
			West	♣	9 5 2

West	North	East	South	♠	A J 8 5 4
1♠	Pass	Pass	Dble	♡	Q J 10
Pass	2♡	Pass	3NT	◇	Q J 2
End				♣	Q 3

Against South's 3NT you lead the ♠5, which is covered by the ♠9, ♠10 and won by declarer's king. At trick two declarer plays the ♣A. Plan the defence.

80

♠	A Q 3	North			
♡	6				
◇	8 7 4 3				
♣	Q J 7 6 2			East	

West	North	East	South	♠	8 7 2
—	—	—	1♠	♡	A 9 8 2
Pass	2♠	Pass	2NT	◇	K Q J
Pass	3NT	End		♣	8 4 3

West leads the ♡5. You play the ace and declarer plays the three. How do you proceed?

81

			North	♠	Q 9 4 3 2
				♡	9 5 4 3
				◇	Q 10 9
			West	♣	2

West	North	East	South	♠	K 8 5
—	—	—	1♡	♡	A
2♣	4♡	End		◇	8 4 2
				♣	A K 8 7 5 3

You lead the ♣A on which partner plays the ♣4 and declarer the ♣6. What now?

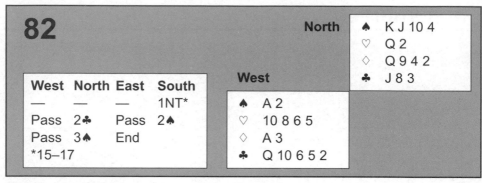

82

West	North	East	South
—	—	—	1NT*
Pass	2♣	Pass	2♠
Pass	3♠	End	
*15–17			

North
♠ K J 10 4
♡ Q 2
◇ Q 9 4 2
♣ J 8 3

West
♠ A 2
♡ 10 8 6 5
◇ A 3
♣ Q 10 6 5 2

You decide on the attacking opening lead of the ◇A. Partner encourages with the ◇10, so you continue with another diamond. Partner wins with the ◇K and continues with the ◇8 for you ruff (declarer playing the ◇5, ◇6 and ◇7). Play on from here.

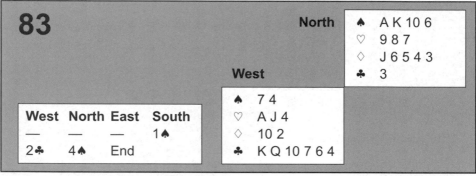

83

West	North	East	South
—	—	—	1♠
2♣	4♠	End	

North
♠ A K 10 6
♡ 9 8 7
◇ J 6 5 4 3
♣ 3

West
♠ 7 4
♡ A J 4
◇ 10 2
♣ K Q 10 7 6 4

You lead the ♣K which declarer wins with the ♣A, partner playing the ♣5. Declarer leads a spade to the king and a diamond to his queen, partner playing the ◇8. Then a spade to dummy's ace, followed by another diamond. This time partner plays the ◇9 and declarer the ◇7. What is going on?

84

North
♠ 5 4 2
♡ A 5 4 2
◇ K 5 3
♣ K J 10

East
♠ K 9
♡ K 9
◇ Q J 9 4
♣ 9 8 6 5 4

West	North	East	South
—	—	—	1♡
Pass	3♡	Pass	3NT
End			

West leads the ♠Q. You overtake with the ♠K and return the ♠9. Partner overtakes with the ♠J and continues with the ♠10. How do you defend?

Solutions

79 If you don't play your ♣Q under declarer's ace you will be sunk. He will cross to dummy's ◇K and lead another club. When East plays the ♣10, declarer will duck and you will be forced to win your ♣Q. If you unblock the ♣Q, partner will win a trick in the suit and will be able to lead a spade through declarer's ♠Q-7.

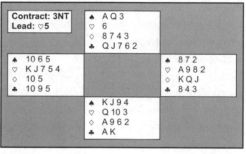

80 While you would generally return your fourth highest in this situation, if you do that here you will block the heart suit. Here you must return the ♡9 and hope that partner works it out. On the bidding, partner can tell that declarer only has three hearts – he is known to have only four spades and with 4-4 in the majors he would have opened 1♡, not 1♠.

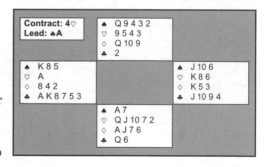

81 You must cash your ♡A before continuing with another minor-suit card. If you simply continue with the ♣K, say, declarer will ruff and play three rounds of diamonds, finessing your partner's king. Now a trump endplays you into playing a spade. If you cash the ♡A first you can no longer be endplayed.

82 Your aggressive opening lead seems to have paid off. It looks as if partner's ◇8 is his only remaining diamond (he can't have the ◇J or he would have played it at trick one). A heart switch seems safest, but it is important that you remember to cash the ♠A before getting off lead. Otherwise, when the layout is as it is declarer will win two heart tricks and then play a spade, and you will be endplayed to lead away from your ♣Q.

Contract: 3♠	♠ K J 10 4	
Lead: ◇A	♡ Q 2	
	◇ Q 9 4 2	
	♣ J 8 3	
♠ A 2		♠ 7 6 3
♡ 10 8 6 5		♡ K 9 7 4 3
◇ A 3		◇ K 10 8
♣ Q 10 6 5 2		♣ 9 4
	♠ Q 9 8 5	
	♡ A J	
	◇ J 7 6 5	
	♣ A K 7	

83 The answer is that you have been asleep and let declarer get away with murder, and there is nothing you can do – not now. You should have unblocked your ◇10 on the first round of the suit. Then declarer would not have been able to duck a diamond into your hand. Partner would have won the second or third diamond and would have switched to a high heart, enabling your side to take three heart tricks. But now declarer can discard two hearts on his established diamonds.

Contract: 4♠	♠ A K 10 6	
Lead: ♣K	♡ 9 8 7	
	◇ J 6 5 4 3	
	♣ 3	
♠ 7 4		♠ 9 8 2
♡ A J 4		♡ Q 10 6 2
◇ 10 2		◇ K 9 8
♣ K Q 10 7 6 4		♣ J 8 5
	♠ Q J 5 3	
	♡ K 5 3	
	◇ A Q 7	
	♣ A 9 2	

84 It looks as if declarer started with A-x-x in spades and has ducked two rounds. Partner's ♠J (his highest remaining) suggests heart values, so you should discard your ♡K on the ♠J. Declarer has only eight tricks without losing the lead in hearts, which will enable partner to cash his spades. Note that declarer was rather careless to duck the second spade, and so give you the opportunity to unblock. Better play is to win the second spade and cross to dummy in clubs to lead a low heart from the table. You now have to play low smoothly. Declarer will win his queen and has to guess whether you started with K-x (in which case he needs to duck a heart now), or K-x-x (in which case he must play ace and another). But at least he has a chance to make his contract.

Contract: 3NT	♠ 5 4 2	
Lead: ♠Q	♡ A 5 4 2	
	◇ K 5 3	
	♣ K J 10	
♠ Q J 10 8 3		♠ K 9
♡ J 10 8		♡ K 9
◇ 10 8 7		◇ Q J 9 4
♣ 3 2		♣ 9 8 6 5 4
	♠ A 7 6	
	♡ Q 7 6 3	
	◇ A 6 2	
	♣ A Q 7	

Chapter Fifteen

Helping Partner

- **Deliberately Misleading Partner**
- **Removing His Losing Options**

It is often the case that one defender knows more than the other about declarer's hand and thus has the best chance of beating his contract. If that is the case, that defender should be quick to take charge and direct the defence towards the winning sequence of plays.

Deliberately Misleading Partner

Some defenders are unduly worried about being too helpful to declarer. These defenders always win with the king when they hold the king-queen. But this play usually backfires because partner misdefends, not being able to imagine the actual layout. These defenders hate giving partner an accurate count of the hand for fear that it will help declarer. I strongly disapprove of these antics. A strong bridge partnership needs to be built on trust – trust that partner is first and foremost trying to help you. Maybe declarer will occasionally be helped by your honest carding, but much more often it will be the way to help partner defend accurately. If partner stops trusting your cards, then your defence will never improve.

In this section I am not going to discuss the type of misleading defence mentioned in the above paragraph, but rather a constructive sort of deception that aims to mislead partner into doing exactly what you want him to do.

Mislead him about distribution

Look at the following layout:

> Take every opportunity to stop partner making a mistake.

(1)

♠ 6 5
♡ Q 8 7

♠ 9 8 3
♡ K 6 5 4

Suppose declarer is playing in a heart contract and your hopes of defensive tricks in the minor suits are limited. If partner leads the ♠A-K, you would do well to play the ♠9 followed by the ♠3. Partner will now surely play a third round of spades and declarer is likely to ruff high in the dummy, and your ♡K, which otherwise could have been picked up, will now score a trick. If instead you follow honestly by playing the ♠3 and then the ♠8, partner may not continue with a third round of the suit, and even if he does, declarer is unlikely to ruff.

Now look at the opposite situation:

(2)

♠ 6 5
♡ Q 8 7

♠ 8 3
♡ 6 5 4

Here you know that you cannot overruff the dummy whatever declarer does, so it cannot help the defence for partner to continue with the suit. It may even do positive harm. If partner continues with this suit and you do not overruff the dummy, then declarer will know that you do not have the king and may drop it singleton in partner's hand. The best you can do is play your small spade at trick one and hope that partner switches.

Mislead him about your honour cards

If you win a trick with the king partner will assume you do not have the queen; if you win with the ace he will assume you do not have the king. As mentioned above, this can cause him to go wrong and is not generally considered to be a good idea. But, as usual, there are exceptions. If you win a trick with a higher-than-necessary honour, you will dissuade partner from continuing that suit when he next gets the lead. Sometimes that is what you want to do.

> If you can see the way to beat a contract don't leave it to partner.

♠ A J 3
♡ 7 3

 ♠ K Q 2
♡ Q J 10 9 8 4

Perhaps South has opened 1NT and been left to play there. Partner leads the ♠6 and declarer plays low from dummy. If you win with the ♠Q and return the ♡Q, perhaps declarer will play the king and partner the ace. Imagine your frustration when partner continues with a low spade and not a heart. But how was partner to know that the layout was not:

♠ A J 3
♡ 7 3

 ♠ K Q 9 8 2
♡ Q J 4

The answer is to win with the king of spades not the queen.

Removing His Losing Options

Often there comes a moment in the defence of a hand when you can relax, when you know that the contract is going down. That is time to take a second look and ask yourself whether partner is in possession of the same information. And if there is a danger that he is not in the same happy position of knowledge as you, that is the time to try your hardest to help him. Here are a few common situations:

Rule of Eleven

If you are the defender not on lead, the Rule of Eleven (see page 19) can sometimes tell you that the suit that partner has led is cashing. But partner may not know this and you may need to be creative to make sure he defends correctly.

Don't let him duck

When dummy has a long suit headed by the king, if declarer leads towards the dummy partner may well duck in order to make it harder for declarer to develop that suit. In general this is good defence, but sometimes he may be ducking the setting trick. If you can see sufficient defensive tricks if partner wins his ace, then you should consider switching to this suit to force partner to take his ace.

Take charge

If you can see how to beat a contract for certain, then you should take charge of the defence. If you know what to do, then be positive and be prepared to ruff his winner or overtake his winners. Don't let him make a mistake.

Try it Yourself

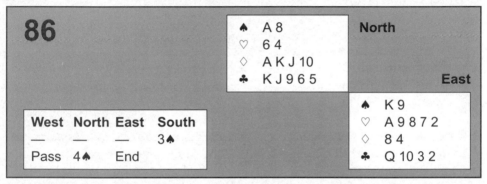

85

	♠	10 8 7 4 3	**North**
	♡	Q J 6	
	◇	A 7	
	♣	Q J 4	**East**

East:
♠ 6 5
♡ 9 8 7 3
◇ K 10 6 4
♣ A K 5

West	North	East	South
—	—	—	1♠
Pass	3♠	End	

Partner leads the ♣7 and declarer plays the ♣Q from dummy. How do you defend?

86

	♠	A 8	**North**
	♡	6 4	
	◇	A K J 10	
	♣	K J 9 6 5	**East**

East:
♠ K 9
♡ A 9 8 7 2
◇ 8 4
♣ Q 10 3 2

West	North	East	South
—	—	—	3♠
Pass	4♠	End	

Partner leads the ♡K. You encourage with the ♡9 and partner continues with the ♡Q. Plan the defence.

87

	♠	K 6	**North**
	♡	A K 6 3	
	◇	10 6 4 3	
	♣	9 7 3	**East**

East:
♠ 7 5 4 3
♡ Q J 9 8 4
◇ 7
♣ K J 8

West	North	East	South
—	—	—	1NT*
Pass	2♣	Pass	2◇
Pass	3NT	End	
*15–17			

West leads the ♣5 to your king and declarer's ace. Declarer cashes the ◇A-K. What do you discard and why?

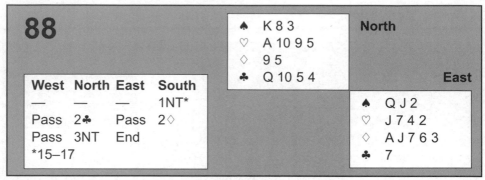

West leads the ◇4 against 3NT. You win the ace as declarer plays the two. Can you see a potential problem here?

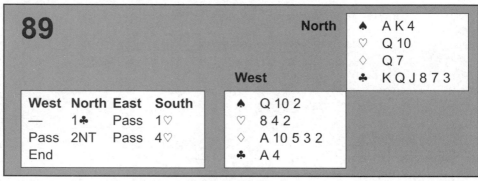

You decide on the attacking lead of the ♣A, which seems to set up a lot of tricks for dummy. Partner plays the ♣5 at trick one and declarer the ♣2. How do you proceed?

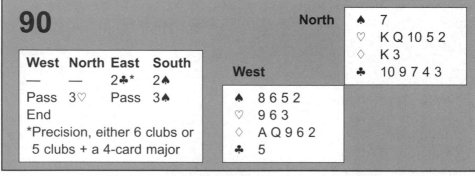

You lead your singleton club against 3♠. Partner wins the ♣Q and cashes the ♣A, declarer following with the ♣6 and ♣J. Plan the defence.

Solutions

85 You would like to put partner in so he can switch to a diamond. Since you do not want to set up too many side-suit tricks for declarer, it looks right to switch to a trump. However, if you win the ♣K and switch to a trump, partner might think you have ♣A-K-10 and play another club. In order to stop him doing this you should win the ♣A, not the ♣K. Now there will be no reason for him to return to clubs.

Contract: 3♠	♠ 10 8 7 4 3	
Lead: ♣7	♡ Q J 6	
	◇ A 7	
	♣ Q J 4	
♠ A		♠ 6 5
♡ A 10 4 2		♡ 9 8 7 3
◇ J 9 8 5 3		◇ K 10 6 4
♣ 8 7 2		♣ A K 5
	♠ K Q J 9 2	
	♡ K 5	
	◇ Q 2	
	♣ 10 9 6 3	

86 You should overtake the ♡Q with your ace and lead a club. Partner does not know that you hold the ♠K – indeed he will imagine that declarer does not have a trump loser. He may well decide to underlead his ♣A at trick three in order to put declarer to a guess for his contract. That is the last thing you want him to do, so stop him doing it by overtaking and playing a club yourself.

Contract: 4♠	♠ A 8	
Lead: ♡K	♡ 6 4	
	◇ A K J 10	
	♣ K J 9 6 5	
♠ 5		♠ K 9
♡ K Q J		♡ A 9 8 7 2
◇ Q 9 7 5 3 2		◇ 8 4
♣ A 8 7		♣ Q 10 3 2
	♠ Q J 10 7 6 4 3 2	
	♡ 10 5 3	
	◇ 6	
	♣ 4	

87 If you use your Rule of Eleven, you will work out that partner must have started out with Q-10-6-5(-x) in clubs, most likely a five-card suit for declarer would probably have ducked at trick one if he had started with A-x-x. So you know the club suit is running, but partner does not. He does not know who has the ♣J. You should tell him that declarer does not have the ♣J – by discarding it! Now when partner wins the ◇Q there is no risk of him trying to put you in – he will simply cash his clubs.

Contract: 3NT	♠ K 6	
Lead: ♣5	♡ A K 6 3	
	◇ 10 6 4 3	
	♣ 9 7 3	
♠ Q J 9 8		♠ 7 5 4 3
♡ 5		♡ Q J 9 8 4
◇ Q 8 2		◇ 7
♣ Q 10 6 5 2		♣ K J 8
	♠ A 10 2	
	♡ 10 7 2	
	◇ A K J 9 5	
	♣ A 4	

88 If you make the normal play of winning the ◇A and returning the ◇6, there is a real risk that partner will think you started with ◇A-6-3. If that is the case, because he does not have an entry, his best play is to duck declarer's ◇Q, so that when you next gain the lead you can play

Contract: 3NT Lead: ◇4	♠ K 8 3 ♡ A 10 9 5 ◇ 9 5 ♣ Q 10 5 4	
♠ 10 7 6 5 ♡ Q 6 ◇ K 10 8 4 ♣ J 8 3		♠ Q J 2 ♡ J 7 4 2 ◇ A J 7 6 3 ♣ 7
	♠ A 9 4 ♡ K 8 3 ◇ Q 2 ♣ A K 9 6 2	

another diamond through declarer's supposed remaining J-7. If you tell him a lie for his own good, by returning the ◇3 instead, he cannot go wrong.

89 Maybe your opening lead was not such a good idea, but it is too late to take it back. Even if you can develop a spade trick, surely declarer will have enough tricks before you can get in to cash it. But maybe your ♡8 can prove to be an embarrassment. You have to hope that partner has a

Contract: 4♡ Lead: ♣A	♠ A K 4 ♡ Q 10 ◇ Q 7 ♣ K Q J 8 7 3	
♠ Q 10 2 ♡ 8 4 2 ◇ A 10 5 3 2 ♣ A 4		♠ J 9 8 7 3 ♡ K J ◇ J 9 6 ♣ 10 6 5
	♠ 6 5 ♡ A 9 7 6 5 3 ◇ K 8 4 ♣ 9 2	

significant doubleton heart – perhaps K-J or A-J. Now if you play a second club and he plays a third when he gets in with his trump trick, your ♡8 will be promoted. However, you should cash the ◇A first. Partly so that partner can cash his ◇K if he has it, and partly so that he knows there is no need to play a diamond through declarer. Note that your opening lead and subsequent defence was the only way to beat 4♡.

90 It looks as if declarer has a very good spade suit and that your partner has the ♡A. If that is the case, you *know* how to beat 3♠. Because you know partner has only a five-card club suit, you know he has four hearts and declarer surely has at least three diamonds. Rather than leave it to

Contract: 3♠ Lead: ♣5	♠ 7 ♡ K Q 10 5 2 ◇ K 3 ♣ 10 9 7 4 3	
♠ 8 6 5 2 ♡ 9 6 3 ◇ A Q 9 6 2 ♣ 5		♠ 4 ♡ A J 8 4 ◇ J 7 4 ♣ A K Q 8 2
	♠ A K Q J 10 9 3 ♡ 7 ◇ 10 8 5 ♣ J 6	

partner, who may think he should be continuing clubs to promote your trump tricks, take charge yourself. Ruff your partner's club winner at trick two and return a low diamond. Declarer will probably win with dummy's king and play the ♡K. Now your partner can win and return a diamond. You win and play a trump and the hand is over.

Chapter Sixteen

Helping Declarer Go Wrong

- **Playing the Card You are Known to Hold**
- **Giving Declarer a Losing Option**
- **Making Declarer Guess Early**

Just as sometimes you have to use deception to help partner find the right defence, there are other times when you can see that, left to his own devices, declarer cannot help but succeed. At such times you have to use your imagination and put yourself in his shoes. Ask yourself the question: 'Is there any way I can persuade declarer that the layout is different from what it actually is?'

Playing the Card You are Known to Hold

Suppose this is the layout of a suit:

```
              A J 5
   Q 10 2    [_____]     7 4 3
              K 9 8 6
```

> If it cannot cost, always play the card you are known to hold.

Declarer leads a low card to dummy's jack, which holds the trick. He then cashes the ace. If West plays the ten on this trick, declarer knows that he still holds the queen, so it is not very difficult for him to rise with the king on the third round, making four tricks in the suit. Now suppose that when declarer plays dummy's ace West plays the queen, the card he is known to hold; declarer does not know who has the ten and may well play to his nine on the next round, thinking the original layout was:

```
              A J 5
   Q 2       [_____]    10 7 4 3
              K 9 8 6
```

Keep an eye out for other similar situations.

Giving Declarer a Losing Option

Let's look at a few more layouts:

```
              A J 6 4
   K 5       [_____]    10 9 3
              Q 8 7 2
```

Declarer broaches this suit by playing low towards dummy's jack. If East plays low on this trick, then declarer has no choice but to try the ace, dropping West's king.

But suppose that East drops the nine or ten. Now declarer might decide to play him for ten-nine doubleton and cross back to hand to run the queen.

```
              A Q 9 8 6 4
   7 2       [_____]    J 10 3
              K 5
```

When declarer plays the king from hand, East must drop the jack or ten. Then declarer may play him for a singleton honour and finesse on the next round. If East plays low declarer cannot go wrong.

Try this one in the context of a complete deal:

	♠ 4 2	**North**
	♡ K Q 7 4	
	◇ K 10 8 5	
West	♣ A Q J	**East**

♠ A 5		♠ 10 9 8 7
♡ 10 6 3		♡ J 8 5 2
◇ J 9 7 6		◇ 2
♣ K 10 9 6		♣ 7 4 3 2

	♠ K Q J 6 3	
	♡ A 9	
	◇ A Q 4 3	
South	♣ 8 5	

North/South reached Six Diamonds after North had opened One No-trump (15–17).

West found the attacking lead of the ten of clubs and, after a lot of thought, declarer finessed. He then led a diamond to his queen and West played the *nine*. Taking this card at face value, declarer crossed to dummy's king of diamonds and could not recover.

Had West played a straightforward six of diamonds on the first round of the suit, the only 4-1 declarer could cope with would have been four cards with West, so declarer would have had no option but to make his contract.

Making Declarer Guess Early

The good declarer tries to find out as much as he can about a hand before making crucial plays. And he also likes to combine his chances as much as possible, testing one suit and then another. The good defender should try to force him to make his crucial plays as early as possible.

Look at this example:

	North
♠ A Q 6 4	
♡ A Q 5 2	
◇ A K 7 4	
♣ 6	

West

♠ 9 7	♠ 8
♡ K J 9 4	♡ 10 6 3
◇ J 6	◇ 10 9 8 3
♣ A K 9 8 3	♣ J 10 5 4 2

East

South	
♠ K J 10 5 3 2	
♡ 8 7	
◇ Q 5 2	
♣ Q 7	

> Put declarer to an early guess before he can test his other options.

North/South did well in the bidding to reach the thin Six Spades. West led the king of clubs and had to consider what to do when he saw the dummy. It looked to him as if everything was lying well for declarer, so at trick two he switched to the jack of hearts.

Now if declarer had been given a passive defence, such as a trump switch, it would have been easy. He would have drawn trumps, tested diamonds to see if they broke 3-3, and if not he would have taken the heart finesse.

But now he had to decide whether to take the heart finesse before he knew about the diamond break. Although the heart finesse is the better odds, no-one likes to lose the first two tricks in a slam, and maybe there would be a squeeze if West held the king of hearts and the four diamonds. So declarer went up with the ace of hearts and now had to go down.

Try it Yourself

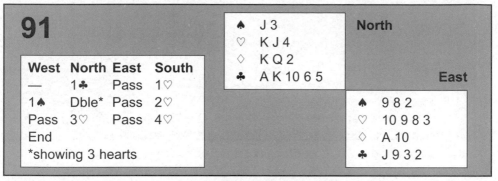

91

West	North	East	South
—	1♣	Pass	1♡
1♠	Dble*	Pass	2♡
Pass	3♡	Pass	4♡
End			
*showing 3 hearts			

North
♠ J 3
♡ K J 4
◇ K Q 2
♣ A K 10 6 5

East
♠ 9 8 2
♡ 10 9 8 3
◇ A 10
♣ J 9 3 2

West leads the ♠A against 4♡. How do you think you are going to defeat declarer's game.

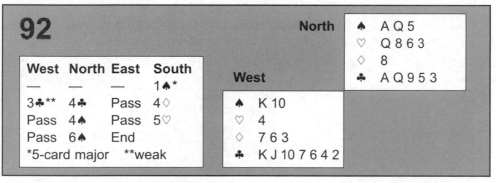

92

West	North	East	South
—	—	—	1♠*
3♣**	4♣	Pass	4◇
Pass	4♠	Pass	5♡
Pass	6♠	End	
*5-card major	**weak		

North
♠ A Q 5
♡ Q 8 6 3
◇ 8
♣ A Q 9 5 3

West
♠ K 10
♡ 4
◇ 7 6 3
♣ K J 10 7 6 4 2

You lead your singleton heart. Declarer plays low from dummy and wins partner's jack with his ace. He now plays a low spade. How are you hoping to beat the slam?

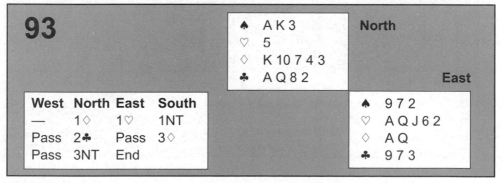

93

West	North	East	South
—	1◇	1♡	1NT
Pass	2♣	Pass	3◇
Pass	3NT	End	

North
♠ A K 3
♡ 5
◇ K 10 7 4 3
♣ A Q 8 2

East
♠ 9 7 2
♡ A Q J 6 2
◇ A Q
♣ 9 7 3

West leads the ♡3. Plan the defence.

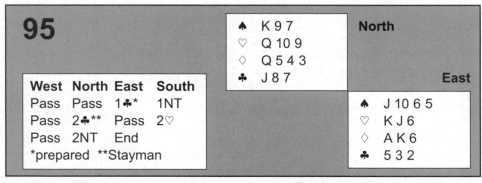

94

North
- ♠ A Q 10 6 4
- ♡ J 8 2
- ◇ A Q 8 7 2
- ♣ —

West
- ♠ 2
- ♡ K Q 10 4
- ◇ K J 3
- ♣ K Q 9 7 2

West	North	East	South
1♡	2♡*	3♡	3♠
Pass	4♠	End	

*5-5 in spades and a minor

At matchpointed pairs it is not just a matter of making/defeating the contract – overtricks can be just as important. The defence starts with three rounds of hearts, declarer ruffing the third. He now plays a diamond to the queen, the ◇A and ruffs a diamond. How have you been defending?

95

- ♠ K 9 7
- ♡ Q 10 9
- ◇ Q 5 4 3
- ♣ J 8 7

North

East
- ♠ J 10 6 5
- ♡ K J 6
- ◇ A K 6
- ♣ 5 3 2

West	North	East	South
Pass	Pass	1♣*	1NT
Pass	2♣**	Pass	2♡
Pass	2NT	End	

*prepared **Stayman

West leads the ♠2 to your ten and declarer's ace. He now plays a heart to dummy's ten. Plan the defence.

96

North
- ♠ A K J 7
- ♡ K 10
- ◇ K 3 2
- ♣ A K 10 4

West
- ♠ 6 5
- ♡ A 8 7 4 3
- ◇ A 8
- ♣ Q J 7 5

West	North	East	South
1♡	Dble	3♡	Pass
Pass	Dble	Pass	5◇
End			

At trick one you lead the ♡A, partner playing the ♡9 and declarer the ♡5. What now?

Solutions

91 This situation was covered in the previous chapter but is just as much a matter of deceiving declarer as deceiving partner. You should play a high spade. You want to fool both partner and declarer into thinking that you have a doubleton. Then surely when partner plays a third round of the suit declarer will ruff high in the dummy and that will promote a trump trick for you.

Contract: 4♡	♠ J 3
Lead: ♠A	♡ K J 4
	◇ K Q 2
	♣ A K 10 6 5

♠ A K Q 7 4		♠ 9 8 2
♡ 5		♡ 10 9 8 3
◇ 9 8 7 6 5		◇ A 10
♣ Q 4		♣ J 9 3 2

	♠ 10 6 5
	♡ A Q 7 6 2
	◇ J 4 3
	♣ 8 7

92 Play your ♠K. If declarer started with ♠J-x-x-x-x, your ♠K is doomed anyway. But you never know what may materialise if you deceive declarer into thinking that you have no more trumps. At the table where West defended like this, declarer continued by cashing the ♣A, discarding his heart loser and then playing a diamond. East went in with his ◇A and played a low heart. Declarer, 'knowing' that West was out of trumps, ruffed low and West scored his ♠10 to beat the slam.

Contract: 6♠	♠ A Q 5
Lead: ♡4	♡ Q 8 6 3
	◇ 8
	♣ A Q 9 5 3

♠ K 10		♠ 8 6
♡ 4		♡ K J 9 7 5 2
◇ 7 6 3		◇ A 10 5 4
♣ K J 10 7 6 4 2		♣ 8

	♠ J 9 7 4 3 2
	♡ A 10
	◇ K Q J 9 2
	♣ —

93 You must play the ♡Q at trick one. If partner has the ♡10 it doesn't matter what you play; neither does it matter if declarer has ♡K-10-9-x. The important situation is when declarer has ♡K-10-8-x, and he is surely more likely to go wrong if you play the ♡Q than the ♡J. If he takes your ♡Q at face value, when you later return the suit he 'knows' there is no point playing the ♡10 because your partner has the ♡J, therefore he may well play the ♡8 and lose to West's ♡9, after which you will be able to run the suit. When you know you have all of your side's defensive values you can afford to falsecard because partner will not get in and it is unlikely to matter if he is deceived. Conversely, it is important to play true cards when you are defending and have very few values.

Contract: 3NT	♠ A K 3
Lead: ♡3	♡ 5
	◇ K 10 7 4 3
	♣ A Q 8 2

♠ 10 8 6 5 4		♠ 9 7 2
♡ 9 7 3		♡ A Q J 6 2
◇ J 5		◇ A Q
♣ 6 5 4		♣ 9 7 3

	♠ Q J
	♡ K 10 8 4
	◇ 9 8 6 2
	♣ K J 10

94 On the second round of diamonds you should play the king, the card you are known to hold. If you follow with the ◇J on the second round, declarer knows that he can afford to ruff low. Then, with the diamonds good, he will cash the ♠K and ♣A and ruff a club in the dummy. He will then draw

Contract: 4♠	♠ A Q 10 6 4
Lead: ♡K	♡ J 8 2
	◇ A Q 8 7 2
	♣ —

♠ 2		♠ J 8 7 5
♡ K Q 10 4		♡ A 9 6 3
◇ K J 3		◇ 9 6 5
♣ K Q 9 7 2		♣ J 8

	♠ K 9 3
	♡ 7 5
	◇ 10 4
	♣ A 10 6 5 4 3

two more rounds of trumps and play winning diamonds. All the defence will make is two hearts and a spade. But if you play the ◇K on the second round of the suit he may be tempted to ruff high. After all, if he ruffs with the ♠9 and you overruff with the ♠J and play another trump he will be down immediately. If he ruffs the diamond high he can still succeed if he simply runs the ♠9, but at matchpoint scoring he may get greedy and play for an overtrick; if he overtakes the ♠9 with the ace and cashes the queen he must go down.

95 If you win your ♡J, when declarer wins your spade return in dummy he will surely run the ♡Q and pick up the suit for the loss of just one trick, giving him eight tricks and his contract. But see what happens if you win the ♡10 with the *king*. Now declarer 'knows' the ♡J is with West and, in

Contract: 2NT	♠ K 9 7
Lead: ♠2	♡ Q 10 9
	◇ Q 5 4 3
	♣ J 8 7

♠ Q 8 3 2		♠ J 10 6 5
♡ 8 7		♡ K J 6
◇ J 10 7		◇ A K 6
♣ Q 10 9 4		♣ 5 3 2

	♠ A 4
	♡ A 5 4 3 2
	◇ 9 8 2
	♣ A K 6

order to pick up a 4-1 break, is likely to cross to hand with a club and finesse again in hearts. Accurate defence will now beat him two.

96 You should switch to a low club at trick two. While it is quite possible declarer is going to take the spade finesse for his contract, another reasonable line would be to try to ruff down the ♠Q and if that fails fall back on the double club finesse. If you allow him to do this he will make his

Contract: 5◇	♠ A K J 7
Lead: ♡A	♡ K 10
	◇ K 3 2
	♣ A K 10 4

♠ 6 5		♠ Q 10 8 4 2
♡ A 8 7 4 3		♡ Q 9 6 2
◇ A 8		◇ 7 6
♣ Q J 7 5		♣ 9 3

	♠ 9 3
	♡ J 5
	◇ Q J 10 9 5 4
	♣ 8 6 2

contract, but by switching to a low club at trick two you do not allow him to test the spades first.

Chapter Seventeen

Clever Stuff

- **Avoiding the Endplay**
- **What to do when You are Endplayed**
- **Discarding when You are being Squeezed**

The material covered in this chapter is included mainly to give you a taste of what can be achieved by expert appreciation of the inferences available to the defence. None of the problem hands are really difficult – it's just a matter of following the thought processes through to their logical conclusion.

Some of the plays looked at here have also been covered in previous chapters, but not at quite such an advanced level.

Avoiding the Endplay

If you can see that defensive prospects are hopeless if you are on lead, then you need to make sure that it is not you who are on lead. Look for opportunities to unblock your honours. Remember that declarer cannot see through the back of the cards. If taking a finesse is the only way to make his contract, surely he will take the finesse. So if he cashes an ace and you have the king, it is unlikely that declarer also has the queen.

What to do when You are Endplayed

Sometimes there is nothing that you can do, but before you unhappily concede the inevitable there are a couple of points to consider.

Give a ruff and discard

> When you are endplayed it is usually better to give a ruff and discard than to give a certain trick.

If you have to choose between giving declarer a certain trick and conceding a ruff and discard, it is usually best to give the ruff and discard. Sometimes declarer's side suit is a 4-4 fit, and the ruff and discard will not help him. Also, in complex endings, he may still have difficulty untangling his tricks when you give him a ruff and discard.

Get off play with an honour

Suppose this is the layout:

```
                  K 10 9
      Q 8 5     [          ]     J 7 4
                  A 6 3 2
```

Imagine that declarer has trumps left in each hand, and you have been thrown in and either have to give a ruff and discard or broach this suit. If whichever defender is on play leads a small card in the suit, declarer will run it round, and then finesse against that defender's partner. He will lose no trick.

Suppose instead that the defender on lead switches to the honour in this suit. Now declarer has to decide whether the layout is as above, or whether that defender has Q-J-x. If declarer respects the ability of the defenders he will probably still guess correctly, because it is with the odds that the honours are divided. However, if declarer thinks you are not up to switching to an unsupported honour, he may well go wrong. Sometimes it pays to be underestimated!

> If you have to open up a dangerous suit for declarer, it often works well to lead an honour.

Now look at this situation:

```
                    K 10 8
        Q J 5     [_____]     9 7 4
                    A 6 3 2
```

Suppose West is on lead and declarer has a trump left in each hand and no side-suit cards. If West switches to a low card, declarer may well play the eight, thinking it most likely that West started with Q-9-x or J-9-x. If West switches to an honour, then declarer is more likely to guess the suit correctly.

Of course, it can be bluff and double bluff. A good defender would always switch to the honour from Q-9-x or J-9-x, in which case, if he switches to a small card he can't have that holding, so perhaps declarer should play the ten. On the other hand, a really good defender might think that a really good declarer would get it right if he switched to the queen from Q-9-x, and so might play low, etc, etc, etc...

Discarding when You are being Squeezed

The mechanical technicality of squeezes is not part of the subject matter of this book. However, there is room for a little general advice about defending against squeezes. Generally speaking, squeezes work against the hand lying under a particular holding. Suppose this is the end position:

	♠ A K Q 6 ♡ K ◊ — ♣ —	**North**
West		**East**
♠ J 10 9 8 ♡ A ◊ — ♣ —		Immaterial
South	♠ 7 4 ♡ 8 6 ◊ — ♣ 2	

If South wants to make all the rest of the tricks and has run off his long suit (clubs, say) he will succeed if West holds both J-x-x-x in spades and the ace of hearts. On the last club, West has to decide whether to discard the ace of hearts (in which case dummy throws a spade) or a spade (when dummy throws the king of hearts).

But if it is East who holds J-x-x-x in spades and the ace of hearts, declarer will fail, for he has to make his crucial discard *before* East.

Some squeeze positions are more complex than this, but most work on similar principles. Sometimes when declarer plays off a long suit you feel the pressure straight away, i.e. you feel that you are being squeezed in all three remaining suits. **It is usually less damaging first to discard the suit(s) held on your left.**

If you and your partner both guard the suits held on your right, and discard from the suits held on your left, few squeeze positions will appear for declarer.

Try it Yourself

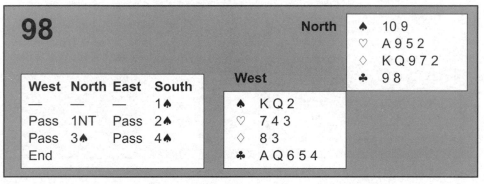

97

West	North	East	South
—	—	—	1◇
Pass	1♠	Pass	2♡
Pass	3◇	Pass	4♣
Pass	4◇	Pass	4♠
Pass	5◇	End	

North
♠ K 9 7 4 2
♡ 5 4 3
◇ Q 6 4
♣ Q 9

East
♠ J 10 5 3
♡ A J 7 6
◇ 5 2
♣ 10 8 6

Against 5◇, your partner leads the ◇3. Declarer plays low from dummy, you play the ◇5 and declarer wins with the ◇K. He continues by cashing the ♠A, your partner playing the ♠6, and playing the ◇J to dummy's ◇Q, your partner playing the ◇8. You are expecting him to cash dummy's ♠K to discard a club, but rather surprisingly he instead plays a small heart. What is going on and how do you defend?

98

West	North	East	South
—	—	—	1♠
Pass	1NT	Pass	2♠
Pass	3♠	Pass	4♠
End			

North
♠ 10 9
♡ A 9 5 2
◇ K Q 9 7 2
♣ 9 8

West
♠ K Q 2
♡ 7 4 3
◇ 8 3
♣ A Q 6 5 4

North/South have clearly just bid a thin game on an unusual sequence. In an attempt to be as passive as possible, you choose to lead the ♡4. Declarer wins with the ♡A, your partner playing the king. Declarer now plays dummy's ♠10, partner playing the ♠2 and declarer the ♠3. What is your best chance for a successful defence?

99

	♠	8 5 4	**North**
	♡	9 8 7 4	
	◇	A 8 4	
	♣	K 9 6	**East**

♠ A Q 10 3 2
♡ J 6
◇ K Q 3
♣ J 7 2

West	North	East	South
—	Pass	1♠	2♡
2♠	3♡	End	

Against South's 3♡, West leads the ♠7. You win the ♠A, declarer playing the ♠J. You continue with a second spade and declarer wins his ♠K, while West plays the ♠9 – clearly a MUD lead. Declarer now draws two trumps with the ace and king, partner following both times. He then plays a diamond to his ace, partner playing the ◇6, ruffs a spade in his hand, and plays a diamond. Can you see a way to give yourself a chance of beating 3♡?

100

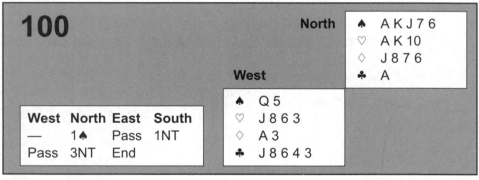

North
♠ A K J 7 6
♡ A K 10
◇ J 8 7 6
♣ A

West
♠ Q 5
♡ J 8 6 3
◇ A 3
♣ J 8 6 4 3

West	North	East	South
—	1♠	Pass	1NT
Pass	3NT	End	

Against 3NT you lead the ♣4 and your partner plays the ♣7, by agreement giving count, while declarer follows with the ♣9. Declarer now cashes the ♠A and plays the ♡10 to his queen, partner playing the ♡2. Declarer continues with a spade to your queen and dummy's king, and then the ♠J on which he discards a diamond. Your discards on this and the next spade are going to be crucial in terms of directing the defence. Can you work out what needs to be done and how to persuade partner to do it?

Solutions

97 North/South reached the wrong game because South thought North's 3◇ was forcing, while North did not.

This deal is all about entry problems. Have you noticed that dummy's second diamond is smaller than all of declarer's?

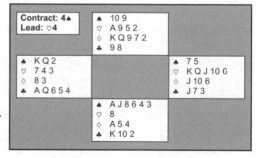

Contract: 5◇	♠ K 9 7 4 2	
Lead: ◇3	♡ 5 4 3	
	◇ Q 6 4	
	♣ Q 9	

♠ Q 8 6		♠ J 10 5 3
♡ K 2		♡ A J 7 6
◇ 8 3		◇ 5 2
♣ K J 7 4 3 2		♣ 10 8 6

	♠ A	
	♡ Q 10 9 8	
	◇ A K J 10 9 7	
	♣ A 5	

First, look what happens if you defend 'normally'. Suppose you play a low heart. Declarer will play the ten and partner will win his king. Partner is endplayed into effectively giving dummy an extra entry. Whatever he plays allows declarer to pick up your hearts. Note how clever declarer was not to cash dummy's ♠K. Had he done so, pitching a club from his hand, partner could have got off lead with either a spade or a club and declarer would have had to concede two heart tricks to you.

The correct defence is to go up with the ♡A and switch to a club. Now partner has a club to cash when he gets in with the ♡K.

98 Surely declarer must have the ◇A and ♣K for his bidding. Along with the ♠A and ♠J that gives him 12 HCP. But he really needs a little more to accept the game try, and it looks as if that little something is a singleton heart.

Contract: 4♠	♠ 10 9	
Lead: ♡4	♡ A 9 5 2	
	◇ K Q 9 7 2	
	♣ 9 8	

♠ K Q 2		♠ 7 5
♡ 7 4 3		♡ K Q J 10 6
◇ 8 3		◇ J 10 6
♣ A Q 6 5 4		♣ J 7 3

	♠ A J 8 6 4 3	
	♡ 8	
	◇ A 5 4	
	♣ K 10 2	

If you simply continue hearts, declarer will ruff and knock out your ♠K. Then you will not be able to stop him running all the diamonds. Even though you know he has the ♣K, your only chance is to establish an extra club trick. But it is not good enough to switch to a low club. Declarer will win his ♣K over partner's jack and exit with a club. Now you will have to win and cannot stop him ruffing a club in the dummy without surrendering your trump trick.

No, you must switch to the ♣Q. Now if declarer tries to exit with a club partner can win and play a spade. Whatever declarer does he must go down.

99 It is clear that after you have cashed two diamonds you have to broach clubs. It is also clear that by the time you have taken your two diamond winners, declarer will know that your partner must have the ♣A – because there are no other high cards left and he must have

Contract: 3♡	♠ 8 5 4
Lead: ♠7	♡ 9 8 7 4
	◇ A 8 4
	♣ K 9 6

♠ 9 7 6		♠ A Q 10 3 2
♡ 5 3		♡ J 6
◇ J 9 6 2		◇ K Q 3
♣ A 10 4 3		♣ J 7 2

	♠ K J
	♡ A K Q 10 2
	◇ 10 7 5
	♣ Q 8 5

something for his spade raise on three small cards. There is no point in unblocking your diamonds to leave partner on lead. If you do that declarer cannot go wrong.

If partner's clubs are headed by A-10-8 it does not matter what you do; you will always take two club tricks. On the other hand, if declarer's clubs are Q-10-x, you can only ever take one club trick. So you must concentrate on the situation where partner's clubs are headed by the A-10 without the eight. If you switch to a low club, declarer will play low from hand and partner's ♣10 will force dummy's ♣K. Now the only thing declarer can do is play a club back towards his hand and put in the eight, forcing partner's ♣A.

The best chance of persuading declarer to go wrong is to switch to the ♣J. If he runs this to dummy, placing you with the ♣J-10, he will go down.

100 In all probability partner has one club honour but not two. If declarer has the ♣K there is not a lot you can do (he is likely to make four spades, three hearts and two clubs), but what about if he has only the ♣Q? If partner plays a low club when he gets in with his spade trick declarer

Contract: 3NT	♠ A K J 7 6
Lead: ♣4	♡ A K 10
	◇ J 8 7 6
	♣ A

♠ Q 5		♠ 10 8 4 3
♡ J 8 6 3		♡ 9 5 2
◇ A 3		◇ K 4
♣ J 8 6 4 3		♣ K 7 5 2

	♠ 9 2
	♡ Q 7 4
	◇ Q 10 9 5 2
	♣ Q 10 9

may misguess, but he may not, so if possible you need to find a better way.

It looks as if partner has three hearts, and it also looks as if he has the ◇K, for surely declarer would have preferred to play on diamonds had he held the K-Q or even K-10 in that suit. Therefore you should play to make one spade, one heart, two diamonds and one club. On the third spade you should discard the ♣8 and when declarer plays another spade discard the ♣3. Now partner should know to play hearts. Declarer will win in dummy, cash his spade and lead a diamond from the dummy. But now your partner can hop up with the ◇K and clear the hearts while your ◇A is still an entry to get in to cash the long hearts. The ♣K will be your fifth defensive trick.